PROMPT

SOCIALLY ENGAGING OBJECTS
AND ENVIRONMENTS

TAMIE GLASS

PROMPT

SOCIALLY ENGAGING OBJECTS AND ENVIRONMENTS

BIRKHÄUSER
BASEL

CONTENTS

FOREWORD

It is the week after Valentine's Day in 2018, the day when a high school in Parkland, Florida, was invaded by a boy of 18 armed with a military-grade-weapon. But this time, unlike in earlier school shootings, something was different. This time a children's crusade erupted out of sorrow mingling with youthful energy. Driven by empathy and ethics, this networked and articulate YouTube generation made its loud and relentless public appearance. It quickly became clear that they are united in their belief that technology combined with humanity is the way forward to their future—to all our futures.

This ethos of tech-aided humanity has been developing for decades all around us. It is no accident that the design community, with its ability to give shape to spaces and objects that express their times and the people who inhabit them and use them, is a natural participant in this movement.

As the abstract world of bits invades every activity, we search for a new understanding of what it means to be physically, emotionally, and intellectually human. Designers, who observe people and accommodate our needs, understand our multisensory natures and our need to fully realize our potential for creativity, innovation, idea generation, and collaboration. Designers of every discipline contribute their specialized knowledge to build networked societies that learn from one another about the human condition in all its varieties of expressions.

As creatures of our small green-blue planet, we are gaining an ever deepening understanding of the fragile environment that gives us life. Not long ago, design was focused on visual appearance and style, often with little substance. That approach no longer suffices at a time when different disciplines are connecting to solve wicked problems that confound humanity in our post-industrial, digital age: problems like gun violence, climate change, and the toxic legacy of that well-known 20th century slogan "better living through chemistry." Now designers include scientific findings, both environmental and social, along with information on healthy materials, the new wisdom of HR specialists, developers, builders, community activists and more, in sophisticated client programs. Employees, in turn, want to work for businesses and institutions with clear and rewarding visions. There is much talk about finding meaning, well-being, and connectivity in a seamless integration of life and work.

Understanding what stimulates our senses has become as basic as exploring our connections to the Earth's rotation and our circadian rhythms. This process is not an easy one. Remember, we spent much of the 20th century removing ourselves from nature, from bothering to understand our planet and its fragile ecosystems, while producing noxious materials, including much of what we surround ourselves with in sealed buildings that connect us to nature as if it were some pretty wallpaper.

The book you are about to read and keep on your shelf for reference explores how designers are connecting people to the places they occupy, and the objects they use. But more than that, the designs shown and discussed in these pages explore our need to relate to shared spaces and objects that say something about who we are and who we associate with. There's also a healthy interest in allowing our rooms and things to show natural wear—an incontrovertible sign of the passage of time made relevant by our lives and thoughts.

This is a new kind of design dialogue, just as the political dialogue whipped up by large gatherings of lively, tech savvy, intellectually rigorous kids. These seemingly unrelated groups may turn out to be natural collaborators in reshaping our tortured world.

Susan S. Szenasy, Director of Design Innovation, *Metropolis*

Susan S. Szenasy, Director of Design Innovation at *Metropolis*, started to work for the magazine in 1985, first as Editor, then Editor in Chief, to which the title of Publisher was added. She has since served on the boards of the Council for Interior Design Accreditation, FIT Interior Design, the NY Center for Architecture Advisory Board, the Landscape Architecture Foundation, and the National Advisory Committee for the Robert Wood Johnson Foundation. She has received two IIDA Presidential Commendations, is an honorary member of the ASLA and AIA NYC, was recently inducted as an ASID Honorary Fellow, and received the ASID's Design for Humanity Award. In 2017, she received a Cooper Hewitt National Design Award. A book of her writings and speeches, *Szenasy, Design Advocate*, was published by Metropolis Books. She holds an MA in Modern European History from Rutgers University and honorary doctorates from Kendall College of Art and Design, the Art Center College of Design, the Pacific Northwest College of Art, and the New York School of Interior Design.

INTRODUCTION

FROM PROPS TO PROMPTS

Given the amount of time individuals spend inside of built environments, which is estimated at approximately 90% for Americans, people are surprisingly uncomfortable and dismissive about the importance and significance of their surroundings. As anthropologist Edward T. Hall stated:

> [W]e treat space somewhat as we treat sex. It is there but we don't talk about it. And if we do, we certainly are not expected to get technical or serious about it.[1]

This book is devoted to space, and it explores the nuanced relationships people have with the spaces they occupy. Much time is spent designing and constructing environments, but much less time is dedicated to understanding how individuals relate to the resulting spaces and the objects that fill them. How does their design help shape people's behaviors and emotions, and how does it promote positive interactions and social engagement? The built environment is more than a static prop that rigidly supports inhabitants. In many cases, it is more dynamic and pliable—or has the potential to be. An environment or object, in many ways, is a prompt, which has the duality of being both a thing and an action that incites and inspires. Interpersonal relationships vary in strength, depth, closeness, and duration, and this same degree of variety and complexity also exists in people's spatial relationships. While by no means comprehensive, each chapter of this book explains a critical way in which individuals relate to the spaces that they spend their lives in, and it offers design strategies for leveraging and enhancing these inevitable associations.

OBJECTS, ENVIRONMENTS, AND SOCIAL ENGAGEMENT

People are social beings, so to expand upon the connection between individuals and their environments begins by exploring the interactions

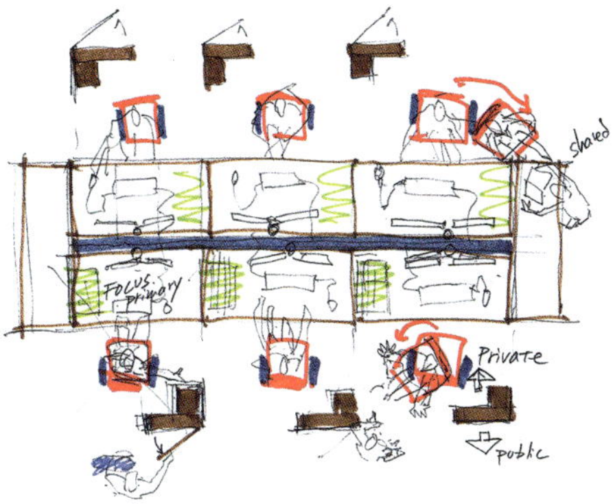

The designers of the Knoll Antenna Workspaces explored the use of "furniture as interface." The vertical storage units, for example, help mediate between colleagues. While defining personal territory, they also encourage courteous interactions. People approaching from behind can knock to announce their arrival and wait to be welcomed "inside."

that take place between two or more people, as well as between people and their surroundings. Sometimes the spaces presented in this book provide the context for social activities, such as a classroom, playground, or restaurant. At other times, spaces and their contents become what engineer and sociologist Jyri Engeström defined as social objects, or in other words, they become the things that spark conversation or dialogue between people. For example, a social object can be a piece of furniture that encourages people to gather or an exhibition that provokes debate. Lastly, spaces and objects occasionally become active partners or companions, the other half of a human-environment relationship or social group. In this capacity, they may help an individual achieve a specific goal or aspiration such as reducing stress, learning to cook, or getting more exercise. It is especially useful in these scenarios to think of the physical environment and its contents as "alive" and actively responding to people.

Before proceeding, a brief discussion is warranted on the distinction between objects and environments. The objects featured in this book, including decorative and functional accessories, fixtures, products, and furnishings, are considered a component of a behavioral and spatial condition. They are presented in-use and not as something to be objectified or observed. All objects require subjects, but this is particularly true of social objects. They have the innate ability to facilitate a shared experience that connects people. Social objects change human interactions within environments, and they can become the impetus for a shift in behavior. On the other hand, people are not subjects of an environment. Instead, they are participants within it, as environmental psychologist William H. Ittelson explains:

> The environment surrounds, enfolds, engulfs, and no thing and no one can be isolated and identified as standing outside of, and apart from, it.[2]

The immersive qualities of an environment naturally increase the chance of interaction. Spaces from the scale of a room to an entire neighborhood are constellations that syndicate objects, surfaces, and atmospheres that engage people by generating and reinforcing social norms, organizational cultures, and behavior patterns.

Objects and environments become nodes for social networks, providing social support and opportunities for engagement. So, what does it mean to be socially engaging? Many definitions and distinctions exist, but in general, there are several essential criteria. It involves voluntary participation in an activity, even if the activity is somewhat passive. It takes place within a given context, which can be physical or virtual, and contact with at least one other person is involved. In an abstract sense, the interaction may be with an object or an environment instead of another person, but importantly, there must be some form of exchange. Advances in technology, such as artificial intelligence and responsive environments, expand the feasibility and likelihood that our surroundings will become even more participatory and active, forming dynamic relationships with people. By exploring the many possibilities, this book demonstrates how social engagement is facilitated and promoted through the design of physical spaces and objects.

HUMAN-CENTERED DESIGN

One may naively think that all design is human-centered. While many believe that addressing the needs, capabilities, and behaviors of people is the primary driver of design, there are competing interests from manufacturers and corporations concerned with cost and efficiency, as well as from designers who prioritize other aspects such as aesthetics and form. There does appear to be renewed energy, however, toward designing spaces and objects more explicitly for people, especially in the interest of connecting people with those around them. Perhaps it is due to the influence of technology, which has brought people together virtually often at the expense of isolating them in the physical world, or to the conflating societal and environmental problems that current and future generations are facing. Whatever the cause, there

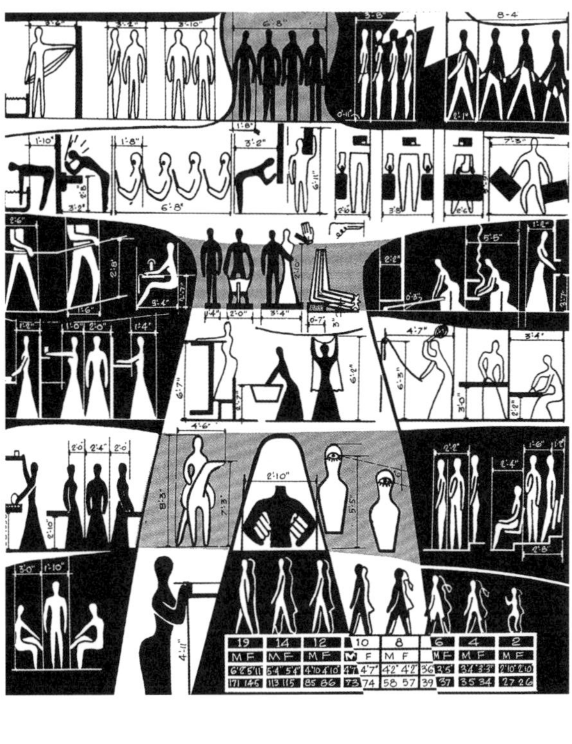

Drawings by Alvin R. Tilley in *The Measure of Man* by Henry Dreyfuss represent average body dimensions and ranges of motion (above). These contrast the illustrations by Nino Repetto in Francis de N. Schroeder's *Anatomy for Interior Designers* which show a social perspective of anthropometrics (below).

is a growing sense of consciousness persuading people to move away from purely consumer-driven or high-design mindsets to one of necessity, usefulness, and authenticity, in search for meaning and human connection.

This is not the first time that society has had these sorts of ambitions. Around the turn of the 20th century, there was a push for simplified living in the United States and Europe, and a movement arose that specifically focused on the residential kitchen as a hub of daily activity and social encounters. Early laboratory-like explorations often dealt with the optimization of this room for women, and there was the belief that transformation of everyday life at the scale of the kitchen could invoke more substantial behavioral and societal changes. This way of thinking about the impact and scalability of design was epitomized by the 1926 Frankfurt Kitchen, designed by Austrian architect Margarete Schütte-Lihotzky, and satirically characterized in the fictional Swedish documentary *Kitchen Stories* released in 2003. Focusing on the residential kitchen and its users was a precursor to the post-WWII evolution, which is expanded upon in Ellen Lupton's essay "Designing for People" in *Beautiful Users*. Developments during this time responded to industrialization and international standards outside of the home that favored efficiency within manufacturing over comfort. Early pioneers such as the industrial designer and author of *The Measure of Man* Henry Dreyfuss popularized the use of human factors, ergonomics, and anthropometrics in the 1940s and 1950s through his endeavors to fit machines to people rather than the other way around. A more humanistic view of people interacting with one another and their surroundings from around the same period was offered by Francis de N. Schroeder, albeit one that still focused on dimensions and movements of the human body. His book *Anatomy for Interior Designers* featured illustrations for interior designers that placed people into various, and sometimes quite comical, social situations. Later, in the 1960s and 1970s, civil rights movements in the United States called for universal design followed by inclusive design in the United Kingdom. Both of these accounted for diversity in people's bodies and capabilities—as well as needs and aspirations—through design, rather than adjusting everything to the average person as in the previous decades. In contemporary times, what is considered normal or average is widely debated, and human-centered design has risen to celebrating extreme differences. Advanced technology has created new opportunities for mass customization and personalization in the design and use of products and spaces, allowing them to adapt even further to the individual.

Concurrent to the midcentury preoccupation of the body's relationship to the machine in all realms of design, Dreyfuss and others began using the word "interface" to describe the mechanisms such as dials and buttons that linked people to the technological devices of the time, for example typewriters and rotary telephones. The focus on improving the involvement between people and hardware and software has since transitioned from interface design, which addresses the way people intuitively determine how to use something, to interaction design where the emphasis moves beyond controls to the dynamic exchange between people and systems. Today, interface and interaction design fit within the more encompassing realm of experience design, a term brought into usage by cognitive scientist Don Norman's book *The Design of Everyday Things*. This approach to design scripts a sequence of narratives around a person's encounters with a product, environment, or service. The way people perceive these interactions, whether positive or negative, is surmised by the memories of their experience.

MODULES OF MOMENTS

Experiences and our memories of them are at the very core of being human. Each person's life consists of a series of defining moments. Some happen by chance, but according to psychologists Chip and Dan Heath, many experiences can be created by deliberately "thinking in moments." Moments are the module—or unit of measure—for situations, and situations ultimately frame the reality of every day. Architects Sarah Wigglesworth and Jeremy Till share their observations about the built environment and warn:

> Any discipline which denies the everyday will be denied everyday, and for this reason high architecture is unravelled by the habitual and banal events which mark the passage of time. There is a thudding disappointment as a gap opens up between the image of architecture and the reality of its making and occupation.[3]

Thus, accepting that constructed environments and the artifacts and products within them, in all of their ordinariness, are ever-present in people's lives opens up the prospect that they could become instrumental in making moments. In daily situations, the surfaces and things surrounding people can play the role of facilitators, creators, and mediators of personally meaningful experiences. For example, consider receiving a text message that says "I miss you," when you are

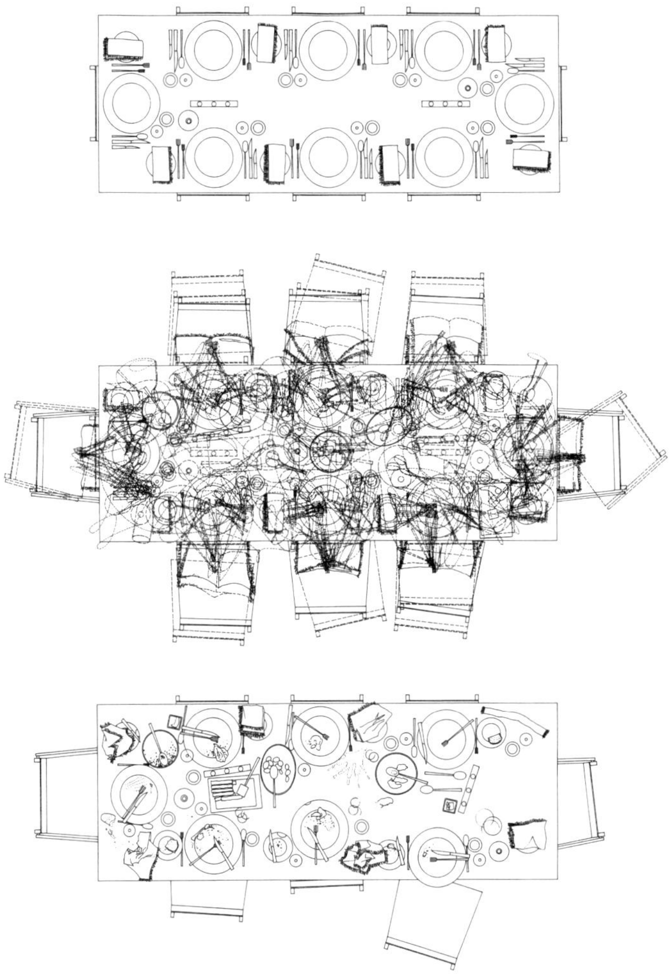

Architectural representation is often idealized, and furniture in plan view does not typically communicate its experiential and social qualities. However, this series of drawings titled "Increasing Disorder of the Dining Table: Stock Orchard Street" by Sarah Wigglesworth expresses traces of behavior, the passage of time, and the general sense of disorder found in everyday life.

far away from a loved one. It may be a tech-enabled smartphone that conveys the message, but it is the exchange and the feelings that it conjures up that is the experience. So, while designers may appear to be merely generating material goods and spaces, it is ultimately their power to provide human connection and positive impact that becomes their value proposition. Don Norman concludes:

> Cognition and emotion are tightly intertwined, which means that designers must design with both in mind.[4]

A designer's ability to activate the surfaces and things in a person's surroundings to create rich, meaningful, and memorable experiences is an incredible opportunity *and* responsibility. This is technically accomplished by identifying patterns of activity that yield desirable associations, studying their structure, and then shaping these into experiences using material form. In this way, designers become the authors of experiences similar to how writers tell a good story. They both build worlds for their characters and must operate within the bounds of what is authentic and natural to these individuals, while guiding them through scenarios and environments. In the end, designers and writers produce something much more significant and powerful than the mechanics of how their work is constructed. It is within this broader perspective that design has the potential to fulfill psychological and social needs, which in turn increases overall well-being.

Meaning and emotion are the primary design objectives in an experience economy, where the memories of events become the product. This idea may have existed long before this term was first used in 1998, but it has since seeped into nearly every area of business and design. In fact, one of the world's largest interior architecture firms, Gensler, recently claimed to have quantified what they call the "X factor of design," where they employ their Experience Index to describe its impact. They call for the human experience to "be the driving force behind every element of a space—from the design of physical space to the qualities of interaction, expectation, and intention."[5] This holistic view tasks designers with assuming responsibility for and addressing the gap mentioned by Wigglesworth and Till before it even exists. While future events are not always predictable, designers can start by writing the script rather than separating themselves from the actual use or occupation of their creations. Experiential consequences, both good and bad, are inescapable, and they do not just go away because a designer does not account for them during the design process. Regardless of design discipline, there are tremendous possibilities to shape people's lives for the better when designers shift focus from the technical aspects of designing a space or a product to conceiving and measuring it in moments.

NOT JUST LOOK AND FEEL

When considering products and environments, it is natural for designers, as well as clients and consumers, to think primarily of their tangible qualities. Even when contemplating the intangible, people tend to

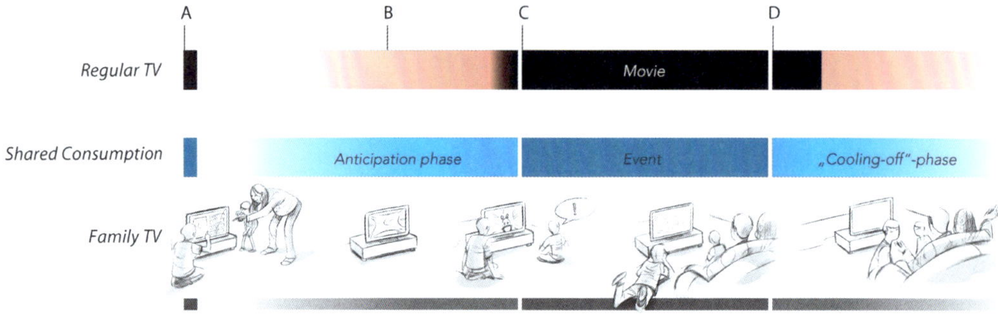

Designing for experience is challenging to represent, because it is activity-based. Notice the similarities of this diagram to the dining table example in the figure on p. 14. Here, the behavior pattern for a shared experience is applied to the scenario of watching TV, leading to features that support the desired sequence of events.

focus on attributes which are still closely related to a space or an artifact's physical form and materiality. Steve Jobs, Apple's co-founder and former CEO, staunchly advocated that design is about more than how it looks, famously saying:

> In most people's vocabularies, design means veneer. It's interior decorating. It's the fabric of the curtains and the sofa. But to me, nothing could be further from the meaning of design. Design is the fundamental soul of a man-made creation that ends up expressing itself in successive outer layers of the product or service.[6]

In the world of software design, "look and feel" refers to how a digital interface looks and how it feels to navigate it. Apple was even involved in lawsuits based on copyright ownership of the look and feel of their operating system. However, this phrase is also used by the likes of industrial and interior designers when generating concepts for products and environments. In these instances, designers will often communicate through imagery to convey a certain mood they intend to evoke. Some designers may regard the practice of employing mood boards as outdated, but the widespread use of Pinterest by designers and the general public alike, estimated at 200 million active users a month in 2017, illustrates the popularity of using a collection of images to capture a particular style or concept. This updated method of creating boards, while helpful at times, may also lead to superficiality and a lack of originality in the design process. Today's image-obsessed population could benefit from moving beyond style and decoration to expand the scope and meaning of the familiar notion of "look and feel."

How does one go about doing this? Firstly, a design's physical appearance or look can be described as character and identity. This type of definition is more flexible, allowing for variation, irregularity, and imperfection. Designers can then focus on what is most appropriate and fitting for a project rather than be subject to predefined stylistic and aesthetic properties that tend to result from design and arts training or passing fashion trends. Secondly, a designed space or an object's feeling can be quantified and qualified regarding its psychological and physiological impact on people. Much empirical research is being conducted in this realm to increase the knowledge base available to designers, but this also requires participation and acceptance from designers. The missing dimension within look and feel is what the designed object or space does—not just how it works, but what it provides or affords people the opportunity to do. How does it act or behave, and how does someone relate to it and interact with it, and most importantly, what experience does the design offer? This relationship between the user and the physical object or space can become the driver of the design, even to the point of leaving the other facets to play supporting roles. In fact, industrial designer Bill Moggridge, who was another pioneer of interaction design and the one often credited with designing the first laptop, discovered that a human-centered approach to design could be so compelling that he co-founded a firm around the idea. Today, IDEO is one of the most well-known innovation consultancies that applies a design thinking methodology to the creation of virtually anything that can be designed.

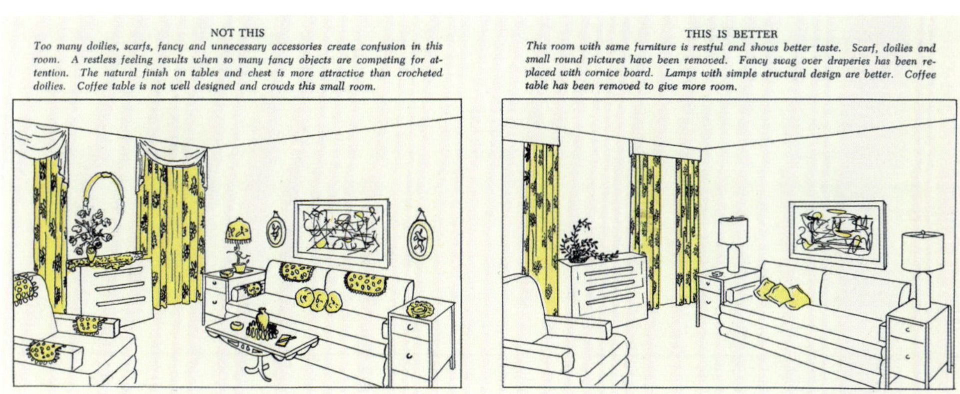

A 1950s home specialist warns about the dangers of over-decorating, noting people will grow "tired of objects which are not in good taste."[7] A further explanation states that rooms should have a "lived-in" look, which might be conveyed by an open magazine left out "casually." This commentary demonstrates how interior spaces have long fallen victim to superficiality.

CHALLENGES IN PRACTICE

The concept of design thinking has emerged across a multitude of disciplines from business to technology and, of course, design; and with this change comes a full range of innovation and strategy design consultancies. These firms, which have often evolved from technology and product design agencies, are now transitioning to designing physical spaces. This makes sense considering that technology is the great disrupter, and it is transforming expectations not only in the digital realm, but also in the material world. Healthcare, workplace, retail, hospitality, and home environments have all been impacted dramatically as a result, and in architecture, this is creating a push toward user-driven experience design. It is also leading conventional architecture and design firms to partner with strategy firms, while others are developing their own in-house training programs to instill architects and interior designers with a necessary new set of skills. While designing for human behavior may be taught across design curricula, it is perhaps more evident in practice when looking at products or cities—but less so in architecture and interior spaces. This strong presence at opposite ends of the spectrum could be due to very different reasons: the prominence of experience design and the availability of full-scale rapid prototyping for products on one end and the influence of extensive

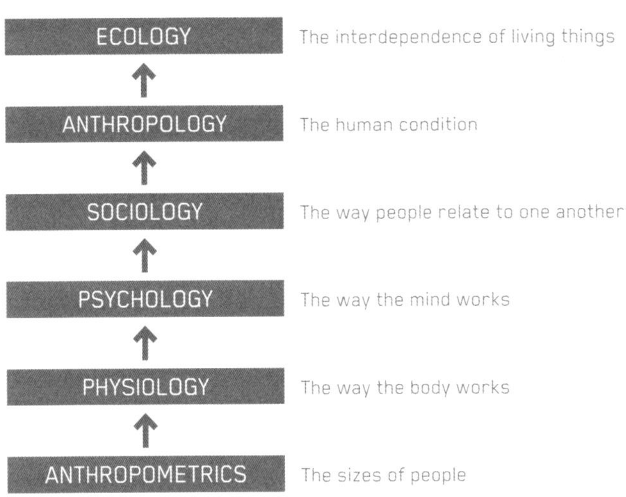

This hierarchy developed for interaction design by Bill Moggridge is relatable across design disciplines. It begins with the simplest of constraints relevant to designing for people and shows how each level increases in complexity.

Model units usually aspire to capture perfection, but a show flat for a keyworker housing development in London by Johnson Naylor highlighted hypothetical traces of real human behavior. Architectural photography often seeks to stylize and mask evidence of everyday life, which is precisely what makes these ordinary images so extraordinary.

social engagement programs for community and regional planning on the other. Generally, designers of built environments are intimately aware of users' needs; but when shaping their reputation, architects and interior designers frequently allow designing for aesthetics, style, and form to undermine human-centered design efforts. The typical architectural design process also contributes to this struggle, since it often neglects the senses, usability, and experience. Furthermore, the mainstream media and design awards still rely heavily on idealized imagery of buildings and spaces, and now adding to this is the pressure to create "instagrammable" architecture and interiors. Simply put, the behavioral aspects of a project are more challenging to conceive and convey than the visual qualities of a design, both during the design process and its documentation after completion. New design tools and research methods, as well as representation techniques and documentation practices, are needed to promote change in the architectural design disciplines. Also of vital importance are new precedents and different language to explain the impact of design.

Further compounding the issue is the great divide between designers and professionals of other disciplines whose expertise is deeply rooted in understanding people, including psychologists, sociologists, and anthropologists and even specialists within medicine such as physiologists and neuroscientists. A fundamental difference between designers and these other disciplines is where each profession's work begins and ends. For example, the work of research-based disciplines often concludes prematurely. They may theorize or suggest the implications and applicability of their research, but their work does not typically extend further. In contrast, designers seem to begin prototyping without sufficiently conducting or consulting research. Without moving toward an attitude of co-creation among disciplines involving research and design, how do researchers understand the realities of practice, and how do designers know that their work is effective in its implementation? There is so much that each discipline can learn from the other, but differences in educational systems and values, as well as a lack of collaboration in practice, tend to keep these professionals far apart with varying degrees of respect for one another. Bridging disciplines to tackle "wicked problems" is one of the strengths of innovation consultancies and strategy firms. They welcome expertise from all backgrounds, but this way of working is still in its infancy of what is necessary to design for an ever-changing and dynamic world. Designers working in the field ultimately need to apply, test, and validate environmental and behavioral research. This book moves one small step closer to connecting seemingly abstract behavioral concepts with the design of real spaces and objects by explaining and representing theories that will inform and inspire, while sparking discussion among designers and others who study the human condition.

BECOMING MORE INTERACTIVE

Changes in practice also point to another development that is not new but finally becoming mainstream. After more than half a century of speculation and experimentation, the design of the digital and the physical are converging. A group of architects and urbanists from the 1960s and 1970s, including Christopher Alexander, Richard Saul Wurman, Cedric Price, and Nicholas Negroponte, are often cited as being among the first to investigate the use of computers, cybernetics, and artificial intelligence in the built environment. Their work with the Massachusetts Institute of Technology's Architecture Machine Group laid the foundation for the MIT Media Lab, whose cutting-edge, cross-disciplinary work today is recognized worldwide for advancing the way people experience technology. The MIT Media Lab's early experiments investigating room-scaled ambient technology, interactive surfaces, and smart objects precede the ideas and case studies in this book. Notably, their work in this area was taking place in the late 1990s, as architectural education was just beginning to embrace the widespread use of computer-aided design (CAD) software. Two

At Amazon Go, there is no cashier or even a self-checkout. Customers use a virtual shopping cart and simply walk out with their purchases, receiving a digital receipt. It is an example of the paradigm shift taking place where the digital and physical are merging into a holistic experience. This level of integration requires that the interface, interaction, service, and interior design be considered simultaneously.

decades later, the ideas and technology behind these early prototypes are being put into practice and are becoming more accessible and affordable, while architectural education is now focused on parametric design, digital fabrication, and virtual reality. Somehow students studying the built environment are introduced early to digital tools for representation, fabrication, and design, but they are less often taught about the integration of technology into physical space as a means of enhancing its experience.

Despite what is occurring in architectural education, the industry is stepping up to make the connection between digitally enhanced experiences and physical environments. For example, while artificial intelligence emerged as a field of study in the 1950s, it has only more recently been integrated into buildings. Of note is the smart elevator which was debuted by Microsoft Research in 2014. It learns occupant behavior to anticipate when someone walking past is likely to call the elevator and to which floor they are going without ever pushing a button. Another recent development can be seen in technology firms that are hiring architectural designers, and architecture and design firms that are hiring digital experts. The move toward the built environment becoming more interactive is no longer just over the horizon, it is a pending reality. Interaction designer James Patten explains:

> As this trend continues, the task of designing our built environment will be as much about designing the interactive experiences that happen in that space as it will be about form, program, materiality and so on. The fields of interaction design and architecture will become one and the same, and we'll need to work across disciplines and cultivate new skill sets to design new buildings.[8]

Inspired by the art of origami, Ori is a robotic furniture system for urban living that reconfigures and transforms interior spaces. This innovative unit, which can be networked into smart devices, represents the future of dynamic environments that can adapt to different programs at the push of a button or by voice command.

Augmented reality which overlays a digital layer onto a user's view of the physical world offers particular promise, as does the increasing integration of smart objects and surfaces into the built environment. Going conceptually even further is the creation of whole environments that are smart, rather than merely a network of independently smart objects. In this scenario, anyone can virtually assign smartness to a spectrum of dumb objects, allowing the technology to recede into the background with an interface that is always there, yet never present. Imagine drawing a light switch on a sticky note, placing it on the wall, and assigning it functionality, or perhaps rotating your wine glass on the side table to turn down the volume on the television. For now, though, technology is already enabling a full range of opportunities. It is currently possible to create entirely reconfigurable spaces through robotic furniture and to go shopping without ever encountering a checkout, but this is all new territory where paradigms are being tested and reinvented.

In lieu of the built environment becoming a network of individually programmable smart objects, argodesign proposes that interior spaces could become entire smart environments where dumb objects are assigned smart properties. For example, a sketch of a light switch could be placed on the wall and assigned functionality.

This shift will affect our experience of environments in the same order of magnitude that smartphones have changed the way we live and communicate, but environmental applications will need to be meaningful to achieve this degree of impact. As with nearly all transitions involving technological advances, there will be many iterations and necessary refinements along the way and indeed some unintended and unexpected consequences. Because of this, it will be critical not just to understand what is feasible through technology, but to examine and better understand people's relationships with spaces and the objects contained within them. Furthermore, it is essential to continue to investigate how the built environment influences interactions and human connection. For many of the project examples shown in the following pages, there have been earlier prototypes, and there will undoubtedly be ones that follow this publication—but the design strategies are meant to endure. There is also much to be learned from both smart and dumb, high-tech and no-tech examples. As designers and consumers aspire for technology to disappear seamlessly into the context of people's lives, enhancing yet also simplifying them, designers may very well want to look back at predigital environments and objects to provide inspiration and clues on how to move forward in a merged digital and physical world.

HOW TO USE THIS BOOK

As with many books on the subject of design, this book offers a series of case studies. It is a collection of 36 projects presented from a designer's perspective, with some described very briefly and others more extensively. They have been gathered over the course of several years from books, magazines, blogs, and personal encounters—and while they may be limited or idealized examples at times—each serves to

The chapters in this book represent a spectrum of how people relate to objects and environments. There are two holistic conditions that fall at opposite ends, where people can either be in harmony with their surroundings or be intentionally challenged by them. The other categories of stimulation, communication, transaction, and transformation are more granular forms of engagement, representing different levels of interaction and control.

illustrate a point, a possibility, or an opportunity of how design can impact the human experience. They are organized into six chapters, representing a taxonomy of engagement, or in other words, a set of categories of how people interact with and relate to designed objects and environments. The chapters explore foundational theories and concepts with specific attention given to design prompts and social implications. Design strategies are proposed and explained through the supporting case studies, and in some instances, projects become a springboard to address potential uses or interpretations beyond their actual reality.

Readers can expect to learn about projects that exemplify how spaces and the objects within them nonverbally communicate to inhabitants and even physiologically stimulate them, resulting in behavioral and emotional shifts. Other examples describe the importance of finding harmony between the built environment and the tasks of occupants to achieve fit or synomorphy between spaces, objects, and particular circumstances. Additionally, this book explains how users engage with their surroundings in transactional and transformative ways, forging interdependent, meaningful, and even empowering relationships between people and their environments. Lastly, this publication describes how a greater awareness and understanding of people's place-based interactions can be skillfully employed to challenge societal norms and cultural beliefs, encouraging people to pause and reconsider.

While technology does play a role in many of the instances described above, this book is decidedly not about technology. Instead, it is about the material world, people's behaviors within it, and their experiences and perceptions of it. Another important goal has been to pry project descriptions away from visual and aesthetic attributes, intentionally focusing the dialogue on what the design does, while revealing any dynamic qualities or inherent values. Whenever possible, photographs include people and demonstrate occupation or use. Admittedly, sometimes this is more stylized than realistic due to the documentation available for each project, which is a commonly cited criticism of architectural photography. Woven throughout the text are references to behavioral and social theories that offer insights for designers. These theoretical underpinnings suggest foundational knowledge, areas for further discovery, or even shortcuts that can guide designers; but they are meant to complement—not substitute—a thorough, iterative design process that includes design research.

The following project examples, descriptions, and design strategies are what is often missing from books that present psychosocial research. The reason is that they occasionally take liberties which were not granted to the respective authors of these publications. It is essential though for readers to realize there are excellent textbooks and academic papers that provide more in-depth information and explanations of the theories which are only touched upon here. Also, books and articles on design research and human-centered design offer an extensive range of methods that may be utilized before, during, and after the design process. As an accompaniment to these sources, this book strives to help fill a void in design and architecture publications. It is intended as a thought starter for anyone interested in the behavioral and social aspects of design, aspiring to learn more about creating engaging objects and environments.

1 Edward T. Hall, *The Silent Language* (Greenwich, Connecticut: Fawcett Publications, Inc., 1959) 147.
2 William H. Ittelson, *Environment and Cognition* (New York: Seminar Press, 1973) 12–13.
3 Sarah Wigglesworth and Jeremy Till, "The Everyday and Architecture," *Architectural Design* 134 (1998): 7.
4 Don Norman, *The Design of Everyday Things* (New York: Basic Books, 2013) 10.
5 Gensler, *Gensler Experience Index* (Gensler Research Institute, 2017) 24.
6 Steve Jobs, "Apple's One-Dollar-a-Year-Man," *Fortune* 141 (2000): 71.
7 Inez Lovelace, *Livable Rooms* (Agricultural Extension Service, University of Tennessee, 1956) 8–9.
8 James Patten, "The Convergence of Interaction Design and Architecture," *DesignIntelligence Quarterly* 23 (2017): 28.

CHAPTER 1

INTUITIVE COMMUNICATION

DEFINITION: An exchange of information by speech, signals, or behavior between an object or environment and an individual

Spaces communicate in numerous ways. For instance, places and objects reveal reliable environmental cues about an occupant's identity and personality. Even the mere naming of a space is believed to influence its design, which in turn could affect people's behavior patterns within a given space. One could say, the essence of intuitive communication is found in affordances. These are the substantive properties of an environment or an object clearly indicating its intended use without giving any instruction. People inherently understand that a dial offers the opportunity for turning or that a chair provides the possibility for sitting. Furthermore, built environments have long defined zones with easily discernable edges and incorporated landmarks that make wayfinding more natural. The current chapter takes this as the starting point for the strategy of imageability—exploring the fundamental theory of legibility—before transitioning to more dynamic and interactive forms of dialogue. Today, technological advancements such as the Internet of Things (IoT), mixed reality, and artificial intelligence are generating entirely new ways of communicating within settings. Computational information may be given expressional form and presence that can be displayed in spaces, or alternatively, smart technology can be coupled with physical material surfaces and used to shape environments. Altogether, the following strategies demonstrate promising ways of enhancing people's emotional connection with one another and their surroundings. As shown in the case studies, designs that employ intuitive communication can protect occupants from harmful or life-threatening situations or help them to strive toward valuable standards such as sustainability, wellness, or fitness.

STRATEGY: IMAGEABILITY

Constructed environments and even objects possess physical attributes such as shape, color, and arrangement that make them legible as they form patterns of recognizable symbols. These traits, which come together to lend identity, structure, and meaning to one's image of a place or thing, can be described as imageability. Introduced in the 1960s by Kevin Lynch in *The Image of the City*, this theory initially intended for urban design has since found relevance in other areas of design as well. It explains how identifiable settings that provide a vivid and graspable image enable people to move about them with ease. In addition to navigation, these environments also play a social role by tapping into the symbols and collective memories that become the basis for groups to communicate. Although people are flexible and can adapt to many circumstances, there are benefits to having ordered environments. According to Lynch, the integration of elements that promote legibility such as paths, edges, districts, nodes, and landmarks leads to emotional satisfaction, provides a framework for communication, and brings new depth to everyday experiences.

Large-scale interiors covering a significant area are now prevalent across many sectors, often resulting in networks of spaces void of anything resembling topography or landmarks. These can be challenging for individuals as they attempt to orient themselves. One workplace environment addresses this issue by adopting an approach not dissimilar to what people might expect to find in a cityscape (Infocomm Investments / BASH, p. 32). Defined circulation paths with discernable edges create boundaries between different areas or districts. Each of these bears a descriptive name and is identifiable by an oversized dimensional sign that serves as a landmark. Additional floor markings convey messages such as when talking on cell phones is not permitted. This system of naming and signage denotes use in each area and helps to set users' expectations within the individual behavior settings.

The strategy of imageability still applies at the scale of an object or product, even though the elements Lynch defined may change—no longer are they likely to be paths, edges, districts, nodes, and landmarks. Understanding and leveraging what constitutes a common mental picture for a particular group of people can aid in communication. For example, a piece of furniture relies on familiar symbols to help children learn how to dress and put away their clothes in an orderly fashion (Training Dresser, p. 38). By adopting recognizable pictogram-like fronts, the chest exhibits visual clues as to the contents of each drawer, making its intent readily apparent.

STRATEGY: EXPRESSIONAL FORM

The material world and cyberspace were previously separate and often disjointed, but they now merge to the extent that people can simultaneously inhabit both. The reality of ubiquitous computing, a post-desktop model of computing that can appear anywhere at any time, is leading to a reconciliation between computational design and the design of physical artifacts and environments. This is facilitated by the detachment of computing from screens—from the likes of monitors, tablets, and smartphones—and the opportunity to display information within the physical realm. Some believe these environmental or ambient displays hold promise for promoting positive behavior change by bringing previously inaccessible information to one's attention within a spatial context. Advancements in this area are challenging creators to conceive of the intangible as something physical; and consequently, designers of products and spaces are making use of aesthetics and lifelike form to communicate with users in expressive ways. One strategy for ambient displays employs anthropomorphic or zoomorphic cues to impart inanimate objects with visual or behavioral qualities, which allows information to take the shape of a facial expression, a pose or gestural body language, or another abstract interpretation. Social science has several explanations that advocate for this approach. Among them, the familiarity thesis states that imitating human or animal characteristics or behaviors helps explain complicated things to people in terms that they are more likely to understand. The social thesis, on the other hand, elicits a moral sense and maintains that this technique reflects human values and possesses the potential for social consequences.

A light switch is usually seen as a utilitarian object, but the design of one light switch in particular uses a zoomorphic form with human expressions to explain the abstract concepts of electricity, energy, and sustainability (Tio, p. 40). The switch possesses familiar facial features combined with symbolic color changes similar to a traffic light that provide direct and understandable information to children regarding their use of energy and how it impacts the natural environment. Being able to visualize the unknown and connect it to human values helps the younger audience link the cause and effect of their actions and consumption with the health of trees and animals.

Artifacts within interior environments are evolving beyond decoration and function into a means of communication. In many spaces, people are surrounded by objects on display. Sometimes these are meaningful, but at other times, they may only serve to fill a void. The use of stock photography to adorn walls, for instance, has become such a common decorating approach that it can go unnoticed. One set of framed images uses this to its advantage as it visualizes digital streams of information and hides them out in the open (Hide & See, p. 44). Whether it is watching the stock market or following friends online, people have become engrossed by the explosion and availability of digital information to the extent that they often seem lost in their personal devices. Ambient displays such as this pull information off screens and bring it into the environment, placing it in one's peripheral view.

STRATEGY: TECHNOLOGY COUPLING

As discussed with the previous strategy, digital interfaces are developing off-screen with information embodying physical objects. Pairing technology with architectural surfaces to construct environments is taking this concept further, permitting the built world itself to become the active interface between people and the digital sphere. In this way, computational technology becomes a new medium for designers, complementing the existing material palette used to envision and shape everyday settings. It is anticipated that working with layers of technology will eventually become as commonplace as handling other conventional materials such as wood or plastic. When coupling technology's temporal structures and enhanced features with tangible surfaces possessing inherent material properties, the result is a physical assembly such as a floor, wall, or table with augmented abilities. At first glance, architectural spaces that incorporate ambient technology may appear visually unremarkable, but they have the potential to provide an immersive, rich environment capable of offering inhabitants new types of dialogue and information exchange.

Floors account for a considerable amount of surface area within buildings, and there are many criteria to evaluate when specifying a floor finish, including cost, aesthetics, and durability. Rarely, though, is a floor assembly considered for its capacity to sense and communicate. In this example, the combination of a smart textile underlay with traditional flooring materials demonstrates one of the many ways that conventional surfaces coupled with technology can serve as an interface within the built environment (SensFloor, p. 46). Current applications of the textile include sensing resident falls in a nursing home and triggering lively interactions within an art exhibition, but it is easy to imagine many other possibilities.

A prototype kitchen for the future incorporates a full array of intuitive features, both low- and high-tech (IKEA Concept Kitchen 2025, p. 50). These range from a color-coded sorting and recycling system to food storage that communicates with radio-frequency identification (RFID) tags to ensure freshness. Central to the concept is a wooden kitchen table with an internal induction element that is enhanced by technology to become an integrated user interface. A display projected onto the table's surface causes it to spring to life, making it more than just a table or an appliance and turning it into a hub for cooking, dining, and living. This instance of technology coupling can help in a variety of ways by suggesting recipes that use on-hand ingredients to assisting with homework.

Modes of communication have profoundly changed in recent years, transforming how people relate to one another. So, it is no surprise that expectations are growing around how people communicate with and within their surroundings. Unquestionably, the fundamentals still apply, and objects and spaces that utilize imageability retain their value and purpose, perhaps even more so now. As people become adept at quickly navigating digital interfaces on personal devices, they no doubt long for a similar ease of use within the built environment. Pushing technology into the physical realm not only permits spaces and objects to become more communicative, but it also augments the static built context by facilitating different types of active dialogue. Ambient technology enables information to take the form of visually appealing environmental displays or to be discreetly embedded within layers of physical materials. Both of these latter strategies offer positive potential alongside possible negative implications. When should technology become expressive and present within settings, and when should it recede into the background? When a designer elects an outwardly visible form of communication, an important area of inquiry is the appropriate treatment of shapes and forms to acknowledge and respect cultural differences that may exist among the intended users. However, when selecting an invisible means of communicating within an environment, how does one ensure people are willing participants and that ethical boundaries are not overstepped? There is still a lot to learn, debate, and study; but the influence of intuitive communication strategies, notably through digital means, continues to unfold.

INFOCOMM INVESTMENTS / BASH

GRAPHICS AND DEMARCATED BOUNDARIES THAT DEFINE ZONES AND ACTIVITIES WITHIN A WORKPLACE
2015

Similar to parks and cities, many large interior environments require a comprehensible approach to zoning, circulation, and wayfinding. It is critical for spaces to communicate their organization and layout, especially if users frequently change. BASH, which stands for "Build Amazing Start-Ups Here," is an incubator for technology companies to help their businesses grow. This particular workplace is in a regular state of flux, even more than most, as it supports coworking, training programs, and networking events. Centrally located hubs offering places for people to gather and interact anchor the interior. The surrounding open plan has multiple areas equipped with moveable and reconfigurable custom-designed furniture that allow for independent and collaborative work, as well as future flexibility. The presence of

The central circulation path is defined with graphics that are reminiscent of highway markings.

Floor and wall graphics provide behavioral messages, letting users know when to silence calls near a massage area, for example, or where to wait when entering the office.

large casters and exposed hinges provides cues about the ability of the furniture and work areas to adapt to occupants' needs. Three-dimensional supergraphics serve as wayfinding landmarks within the space, while also signaling the type of activity intended to take place in each zone. Visible markings and changes in floor, wall, and ceiling surfaces define circulation paths and the perimeters of different areas.

Color-coded, supersized dimensional "signage" indicates each zone in the office, including The Brewery, The Hatchery, The Factory, Mission Control, and Chill.

1

Changes in surface finishes and types of furnishings help differentiate areas and provide cues on how to occupy and use each zone.

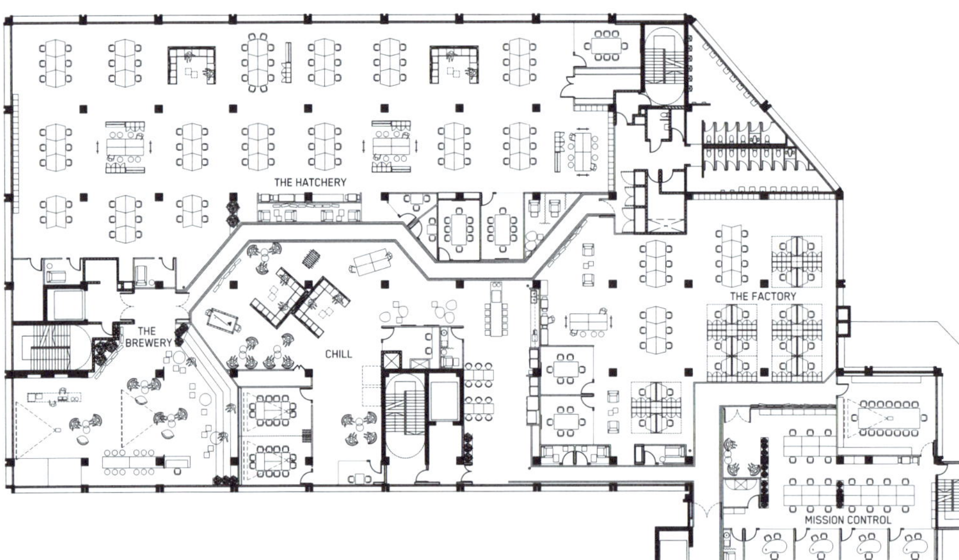

The 2,221 m² (23,910 ft²) space is organized into five zones, each distinguished through defined boundaries, signage, and color coding.

Mobile workstations and booths support different workstyles while functioning as space dividers in the open plan office.

LOCATION: SINGAPORE
DESIGNER: SCA DESIGN, A MEMBER OF ONG&ONG GROUP (WWW.SCA-DESIGN.COM)
MAJOR PROJECT PARTNERS OR COLLABORATORS: BRANDON LIU (PROJECT DIRECTOR), JOHANNAH POSA AND BELNICE CHUA (PROJECT DESIGNERS)

TRAINING DRESSER

CABINET THAT TEACHES CHILDREN HOW TO DRESS AND KEEP TIDY
2011

Cabinets, millwork, and other forms of storage furnishings are typically designed to conceal. Sometimes, we may be able to anticipate their contents based on shape or location. For example, a file cabinet in an office is often readily identifiable as a piece of furniture holding documents. In the majority of built-in and free-standing cabinets though, it is rare that they are designed to communicate what is inside. One only has to think of searching for the cutlery drawer at an unfamiliar house to understand. However, the designer of the Training Dresser opted for a more descriptive approach, employing drawer fronts in the shape of articles of clothing, such as tops, bottoms, and socks. This modification to the design of a typical chest of drawers is intended to help children intuitively get dressed and learn to organize their clothes. Considering the possible expressive qualities of products, furnishings, and spaces may unlock hidden potential for their ease of use and even their ability to inform and teach in everyday situations.

The graphic pictogram-style drawer fronts with cutout pulls assist children in finding and putting away their clothes.

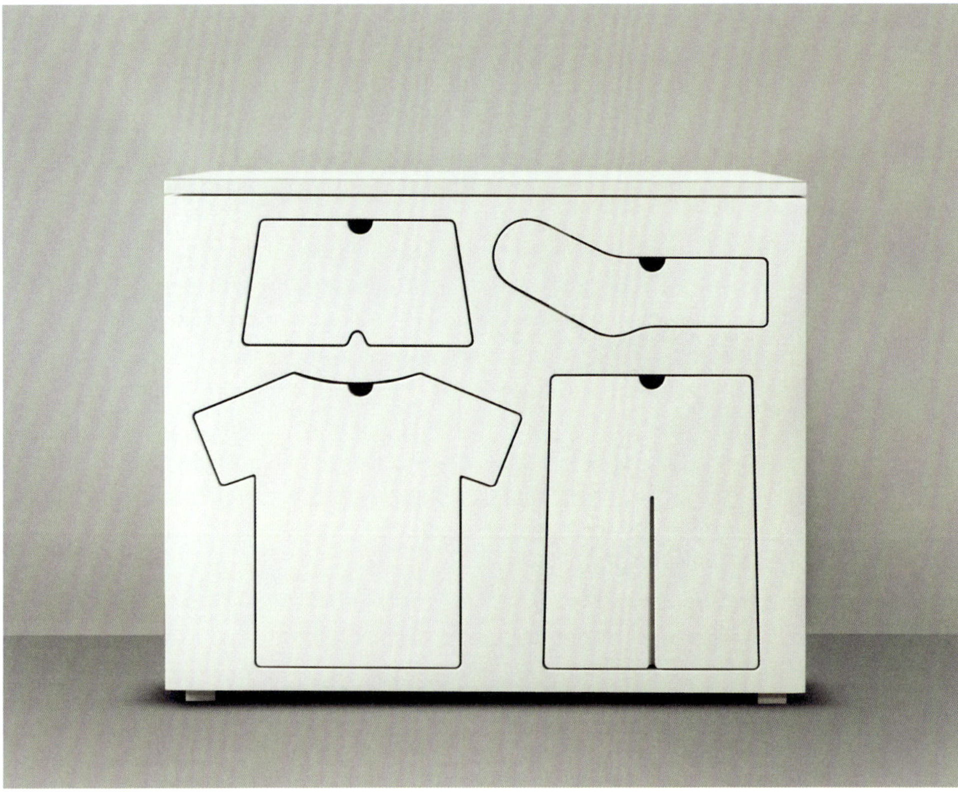

Measuring 94 cm (37 in) wide, 74 cm (29 in) high, and 46 cm (18 in) deep, the cabinet features flush maple plywood drawers with iconic fronts.

The dresser is intended to be understandable and informative rather than a piece of furniture that generically masks its contents.

LOCATION: SEATTLE, WA, UNITED STATES
DESIGNER: PETER BRISTOL (WWW.PETERBRISTOL.NET)

TIO

LIGHT SWITCH THAT HELPS CHILDREN CONSERVE ENERGY
2009

In past decades, parents may have reminded their children to turn off the lights when leaving a room as a way of saving money. While this may still be the case today, there is perhaps more need now than ever before to help children understand not only the cause-and-effect relationship between financial cost and energy consumption, but especially between energy consumption and the environment. Lighting in homes accounts for a considerable percentage of energy usage; and through this conceptual project, the design of a light switch in a child's room serves as a simple opportunity to raise awareness to this issue. With the aim to support and reinforce positive behavior, Tio brings the abstract concepts of electricity, energy, and sustainability to life. As the character of the light switch changes from happy to indifferent to angry, children receive direct and immediate feedback within their personal space about their consumption. They are then able to track

The playful design personifies energy by giving it a face with expressions.

The wall-mounted switch helps children become aware of how much energy they use by lighting their room.

their long-term, cumulative usage online while demonstrating their knowledge of energy conservation to the rest of the family. The software app's gamification feature introduces a playful, competitive aspect where children can become energy champions within their home. Designed in response to a competition brief that called for proposals to educate and empower the next generation to reduce their energy footprint, this small-scale solution is both localized with a physical presence and virtually networked. These two modes of communication are intended to help children take responsibility for their actions.

LOCATION: LONDON, UNITED KINGDOM
DESIGNER: TIM HOLLEY (WWW.TIMHOLLEY.DE)
MAJOR PROJECT PARTNER OR COLLABORATOR: ONZO (COMPETITION SPONSOR)

A web-based application tracks a child's lighting usage over time and graphically relates their energy consumption to the health of trees and animals.

The interface teaches children that they can make personal choices in everyday life that result in positive or negative effects on the environment.

The switch combines emotive qualities with the familiar color progression of traffic lights to intuitively communicate how long the lights have been on and that it may be time to switch them off.

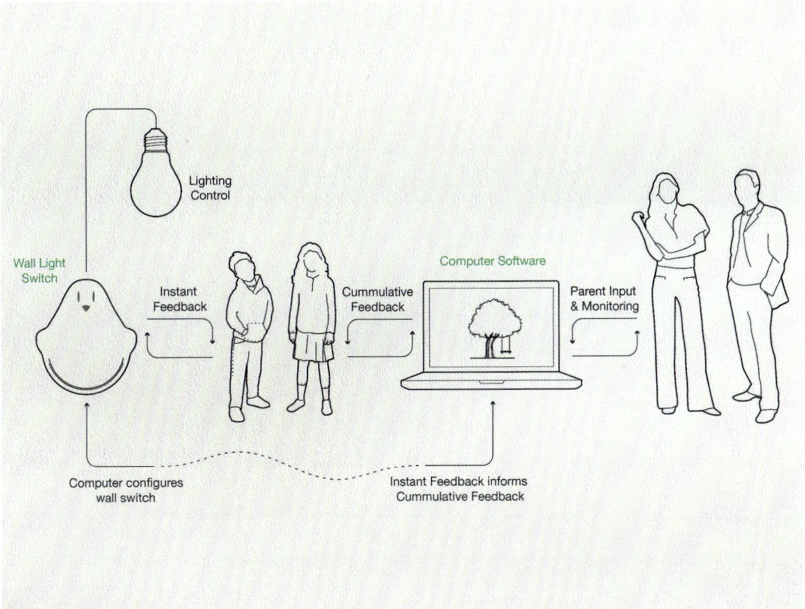

As part of a product system, the light switch sends data to corresponding software, which records and visualizes behavioral effects for both children and parents.

HIDE & SEE

WALL DÉCOR THAT DISCREETLY COMMUNICATES WITH OCCUPANTS WITHOUT ALERTING OTHERS
2010

Interior decorating on many occasions involves filling walls with generic framed images. The increase in retailers that sell framed stock photography and the like is confirmation of the proliferation of this approach. Thus, many environments are overloaded with images that are devoid of meaning in their context, making it understandable why visitors may easily overlook such displays. Hide & See leverages these seemingly trivial selections to hide information within plain sight. Rather than permitting mobile devices to become a distraction in social settings, the designer aims to redirect attention back to one's surroundings. This shift is achieved by coding information into images that are shown on framed LCD screens and intended to blend into the background. A quick glimpse will reveal various flows of digital information disguised as minor alterations of the photographic imagery. Undetectable to most, users remain inconspicuously connected to their digital devices without continually holding them in their hand. Through this thought-provoking prototype, one can be unobtrusively made aware of incoming calls, the whereabouts of partners, children's

An image of a couple walking along a beach contains coded information. Details such as the movement of the clouds, the color of a shoulder bag, and the presence of footprints relay specifics about the location of a partner.

Missed phone calls appear as random freckles or beauty marks on the portrait of a woman. Their location provides subtle cues; for example, dots appearing near the lips signify calls from important numbers.

A frame featuring an image from the genre of stock photography displayed in an interior space communicates with the owner while disguising information from the casual onlooker.

internet usage, the status of critical stocks, or whatever else someone deems essential enough to track. While raising issues surrounding social etiquette, constant connectedness, and personal privacy, this design highlights opportunities for integration rather than separation of the physical and the digital worlds.

LOCATION: LONDON, UNITED KINGDOM
DESIGNER: JAAKKO TUOMIVAARA (WWW.JAAKKO.CO.UK, WWW.HIDE-N-SEE.COM)
MAJOR PROJECT PARTNERS OR COLLABORATORS: GERRIT KAISER AND CLARENCE LEE (TECHNICAL ASSISTANCE), ROYAL COLLEGE OF ART

SENSFLOOR

SMART FLOOR THAT DETECTS MOVEMENT
AND FALLS AND CAN CALL FOR HELP
2014

The Internet of Things (IoT) is enabling interconnectivity of digital technology and the physical world to create advanced communication networks and services. The company Future-Shape is harnessing these capabilities in the development of a smart textile underlayment that can be installed beneath typical flooring materials to transform an entire floor area into an ambient sensing surface. Potential applications range from exhibitions and entertainment to healthcare and assisted living facilities. The system's primary purpose centers on the detection of people. It can determine the number of people even if in a wheelchair, their direction and velocity of movement, or whether they are lying on the floor. Capacitive sensors can verify the precise location of any person or conductive object, and they can even recognize liquids and screen for spills and leaks. This information is then used to control a range of customizable features. Accompanying software expands the system's usability, allowing it to become part of an extensive smart building network. One of the first installations is at a nursing home in France where it allows for 70 patient rooms to be monitored remotely from the nurses' station. It reportedly alerted staff to 28 falls in the first four months of use.

LOCATION: HÖHENKIRCHEN, GERMANY
DESIGNER: FUTURE-SHAPE (WWW.FUTURE-SHAPE.COM)

When installed in senior care facilities or hospitals, the system alerts care providers to any patient who has fallen and is in need of assistance.

Capacitive proximity sensors and radio modules embedded in the 3 mm (1/8 in) polyester fleece underlay track people's movements and relay the information to a control unit for real-time analysis.

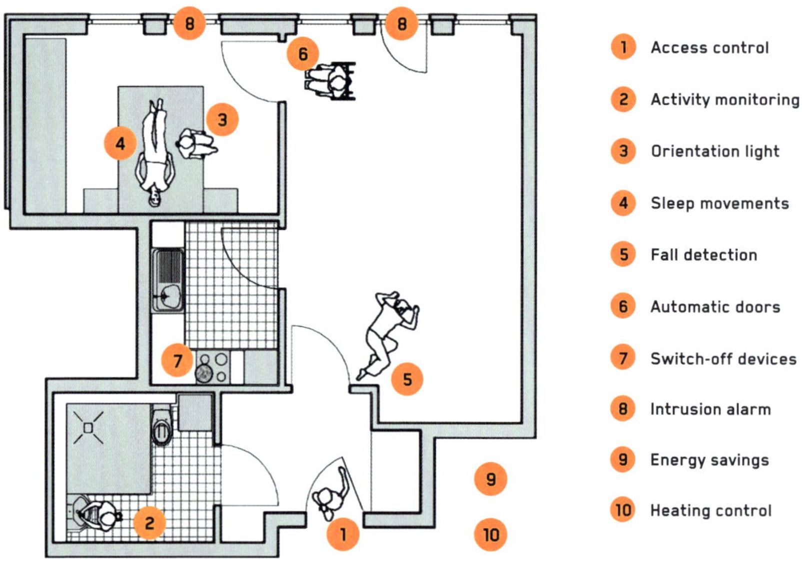

In a residence, the system can extend beyond fall detection to control automatic doors, thermostats, and lighting. It can even recognize an intruder and signal an alarm.

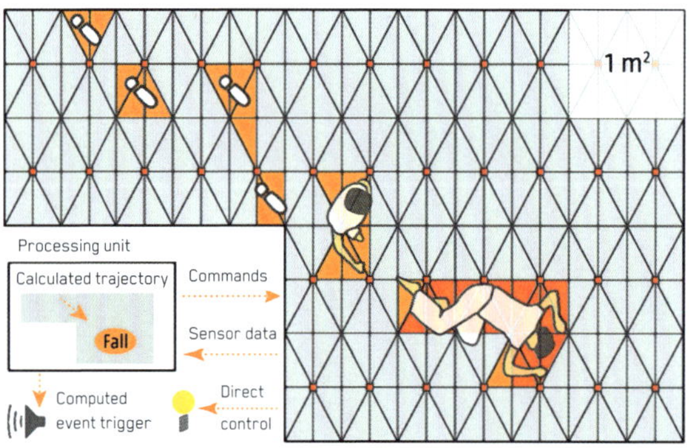

The sensors are triggered by changes in the local electrical field and can accurately determine if someone is standing, walking, or lying down, as well as their exact location.

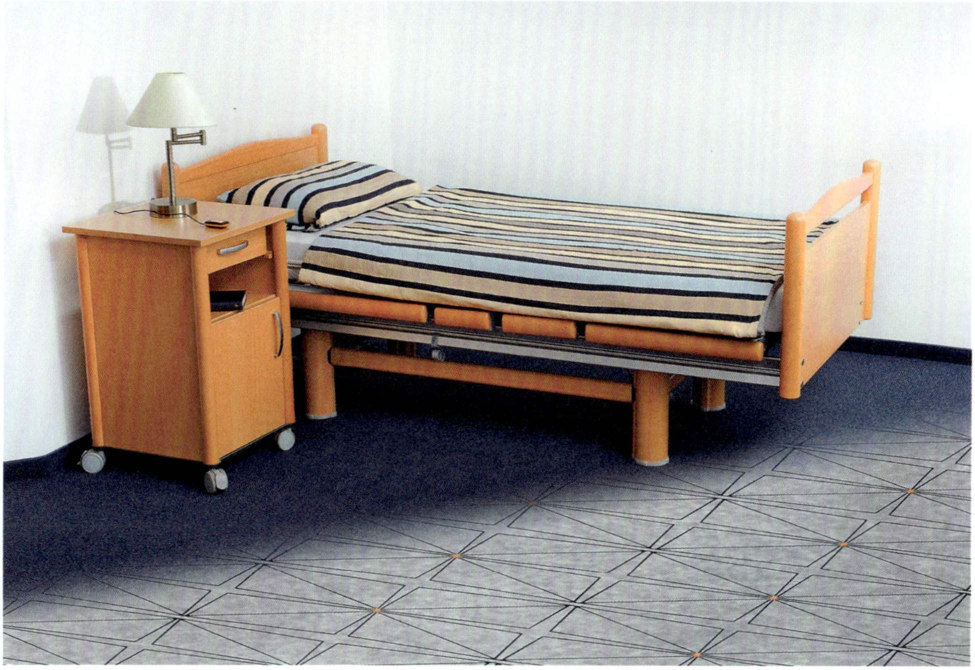

Since the system is not reliant on physical contact, the underlayment can be discreetly installed under most finishes, including carpet, wood, or tile.

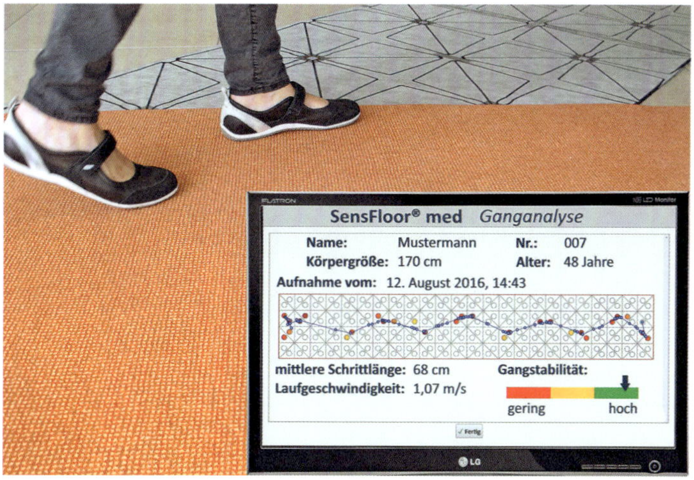

Additionally, the technology can track gait patterns to record a patient's rehabilitation progress or to identify instability so that preventative measures can be taken.

IKEA CONCEPT KITCHEN 2025

KITCHEN THAT TEACHES FUTURE GENERATIONS
HOW TO COOK AND BE LESS WASTEFUL
2015

Kitchens are cultural touchstones; they reflect societal views regarding nutrition and health, waste and the environment, and lifestyle. IKEA, the world's largest furniture store, tasked a group of students and professionals to consider the kitchen of the future and how it could help promote well-being and sustainability. According to predictions, more people will reside in urban environments, natural resources will be scarcer, and waste will be an ever-increasing problem. When grappling with these issues, the team questioned whether people would become more cognizant of food sources or even further detached from them. Furthermore, food delivery is expected to be instant and widely available, and technology will be embedded throughout home environments. With the aim of keeping high-tech features discreet, the team focused on the tangible and experiential aspects of cooking. Their intention was not to move toward automation but to combine physical design cues with mixed reality and smart technology to help users become more mindful about their behaviors involving food. This prototype provides clues to what may be possible in the future and how people may want to cook and live.

An overhead camera identifies on-hand ingredients, and a projector displays preparation instructions and suggested recipes based on how much time the user wants to spend cooking.

The concept centers around the kitchen table, which is where food is prepared, cooked, and eaten. Augmented with smart technology, the intention of the tactile wooden surface is to be helpful, not obtrusive.

Under the surface of what appears to be a conventional table is a series of induction coils used for cooking food and charging devices.

A pivoting sink tilts to one side or the other for the disposal of contaminated "black" water or to capture "gray" water that can be filtered and used in the dishwasher or for watering herbs.

A sorting system helps users separate nonorganic waste, which is crushed, vacuum-packed, and labeled. Organic waste is composted and pressed into dry, odorless discs.

Inductive containers cool contents on the shelves, but they switch to heating when placed on the table.

Pantry and refrigerator merge into an open shelving system to visibly store food. Packaging with radio-frequency identification (RFID) tags communicates with individually-cooled containers employing induction technology to keep food at optimum temperatures.

LOCATION: MILAN, ITALY
DESIGNERS: IKEA (WWW.IKEA.COM), IDEO (WWW.IDEO.COM, HTTP://CONCEPTKITCHEN2025.IDEO.LONDON), STUDENTS AT INGVAR KAMPRAD DESIGN CENTER AT LUND UNIVERSITY (WWW.INDUSTRIALDESIGN.LTH.SE), AND EINDHOVEN UNIVERSITY OF TECHNOLOGY (WWW.TUE.NL)

CHAPTER **2**

SENSORY STIMULATION

DEFINITION: A condition caused by an object or environment that excites, relaxes, or connects people through one or more of the five senses, affecting an individual's physiological and psychological state

Occupants of spaces are continuously experiencing varying levels of sensory stimulation, and designers are forever seeking ways to engage people through the five senses of sight, sound, touch, smell, and taste. Stimulation theories help explain the associated physiological and psychological reactions. From what is known as the arousal perspective, the body exhibits a physical response to the environment that may affect one's heart rate, blood pressure, and rate of respiration, among other functions. Spaces may either corporally excite or relax inhabitants, and it is critical to understand the transition between these two states, or the point at which one moves from over-stimulation to under-stimulation or vice versa. Nevertheless, this sensation is short-lived by an occupant, because people quickly adapt to their surroundings. They then require a significant difference in stimuli for a change to be perceived again, which is a construct known as the adaptation level theory. People benefit from successive sensory changes within their environments for many reasons, but primarily because they break the habituation that inevitably follows each alteration after some time. By strategically embracing sensory stimulation through design, it is possible to heighten spatial and bodily awareness, changing how one feels emotionally. As illustrated by the following case studies, a threshold can become a beneficial sensory transition within or between spaces; specific types of sensory stimulation can provide a restorative advantage to individuals; and finally, shared sensory experiences may become social conveners to connect one another in the material world.

STRATEGY: SENSORY THRESHOLD

A threshold in architectural terms refers to an actual doorway or entrance, but beyond this literal interpretation, it metaphorically symbolizes a point of entering or beginning. However, a threshold in psychology is the strength at which a stimulus is perceivable. Designers may merge these meanings to define the term threshold as the point of transition from too much or too little stimulation within a built environment. With this in mind, it can be impactful to determine a time and a place to orchestrate a change between desired stimulation levels, leveraging the full meaning of the word threshold. Even though people's backgrounds and personalities influence their preferred level of stimulation, generalizations can be made to help determine where to introduce a welcomed shift. Thoughtful interruptions can reframe an individual's mental and physical states, but it is important to note that it will only be temporary. As discussed previously, one will quickly adapt to the new normal, and it will again take another change in stimulus for it to be noticeable. Weber's Law states that the change needed to notice the difference between two stimuli is proportional to the original intensity of the stimulus. For example, if someone places a pencil into another's hand, the person will notice the weight of it; but if someone places a pencil on top of a heavy box another person is carrying, the additional weight of the pencil will not be perceivable. This concept is vital when employing the sensory threshold design strategy. Going well beyond the "just noticeable difference" is imperative. To put this into spatial terms, consider to what extent the sensory experience of a space contrasts with an adjacent space and what is required for an occupant to take note.

Many of today's built environments are overly stimulating. High levels of visual and acoustic noise, especially in public and communal spaces, contribute significantly to an individual's cognitive load. A couple of case studies, including an airport and a department store, tackle the issue by employing sensory thresholds. They accomplish this strategy by providing a secondary space as relief from the primary space (The Magic Threshold, p. 62, and Silence Room, p. 66). While one of these examples is a pass-through space and the other is a destination, they both offer an abrupt change using similar methods to juxtapose the intensity of sensory stimulation offered by adjacent environments. Visual complexity within the secondary spaces is reduced through the use of monochromatic palettes and simple forms executed in a limited number of materials. Lighting and sound levels are modulated to enhance the contrasting effect to their surroundings. A cooling mist curtain and soft felt surfaces offer unsuspecting and palpable opportunities that also contribute to the shift. Overall, these two interventions appear to be purposeless, but once one takes into account the potential physical and psychological benefits of such spaces, their intentions become apparent. Perhaps it is time to propose that sensory thresholds become an essential programmatic component of certain types of built environments.

STRATEGY: RESTORATIVE ADVANTAGE

Attentional capacity is limited and must be restored between periods of directed attention, such as when someone studies intensely for an exam or maintains focus while working on a project. Forms of "soft fascinations" requiring effortless attention are recognized as offering the necessary space and time for reflection to help replenish a person's attention span. Exposure to nature accomplishes this and is a proven method for restoration, which can be as immersive as a walk on the beach or through a forest, or as simple as looking at a photograph of a natural setting. The latter is an easy way to access nature while indoors, which could be useful for people confined to a hospital bed, for example, or who live in a dense urban area. However, this strategy aims for a more ambient approach and considers the possibility that constructed environments could embody beneficial atmospheric qualities. As such, a literal translation of nature is not necessary, but rather an abstract understanding of how to simulate the same pleasurable reactions normally triggered by the natural world. Visiting spaces with a restorative advantage could offer people a respite from the focus that their daily tasks may require of them, allowing them to return feeling recharged until they must repeat the cycle.

One such instance is an artwork that uses sophisticated software and new materials to create an ever-changing interior (Shade, p. 72). Sensors harness the unpredictability of wind and convert it into randomized patterns of light and shadow using a programmable film applied to the fenestration of a building. The dappled light effect is comparable to sunlight filtering through the leaves of trees, but it can be digitally sped up or slowed down depending on the desired output. Interior spaces are often static and overly climatized environments, lacking the dynamic qualities exhibited in nature. This reality is leading artists, designers, and psychologists to explore the concept of "indoor weather" as a way of bringing natural movements inside where people can reap their benefits while being sheltered from the actual elements.

Wellness spas are a typology that is synonymous with restoration. One example is unique in that it oscillates between being a soft fascination and acting as a social gathering place (Liquidrom in Tempodrom, p. 78). The focal area is a central saltwater pool fitted with underwater speakers that pipe in music that is only discernable below the water's surface, where it can also be felt throughout the body. When this concept of "liquid sound" is combined with an overhead light show and the weightless feeling induced by the water's salt content, one experiences a deep sense of relaxation in a short period of time. Few would argue that this immersive full-body sensory experience does not offer potential therapeutic effects. When one visits at an off-peak time with low visitor numbers, they will likely leave feeling calm and refreshed. On a separate visit though, one may join a large crowd and enjoy a live underwater concert, resulting in an exciting inverse effect. The reversing of an inward, reflective opportunity into a highly stimulating social interaction is a fitting segue into the next strategy.

STRATEGY: SOCIAL CONVENER

A simple meeting room may offer a place for occupants to assemble, but does it help initiate conversation, or does it only accommodate? This strategy poses the question of how designed objects and spaces themselves can become the convener. Instead of serving merely as a container or a bolster for social activity, it is possible to convert an inanimate object or space into an active participant. This transfer can occur when a design possesses the ability to bring people together around a shared purpose or experience. Designing for the senses becomes an ideal driver for this approach. When addressing a broad modality spectrum that extends beyond visual attributes, designers begin to conceive of the environment and the objects and people within it as dynamic forces responding to one another. Planning for a shared moment within a project creates the potential for two or more people to find common ground, and thus lays the foundation for a design to become a social convener. Environments that enrich our engagement with physical places encourage people to connect in real-world communal environments instead of virtual ones. In light of the current technological possibilities, physical spaces need to promote a sense of community and satisfy on a deeper level than ever before. Designing with sensory stimulation in mind can aid in achieving this.

Defining project goals in terms of social engagement in addition to aesthetics, formal expression, and function is vital. The emphasis on a particular human-centric aim may very well alter or shape the design process. In one example, a textile designer began with the objective to spark social interaction through the creation of a textile screen (On Tension, p. 84), but early mockups revealed that people were hesitant to engage with the first prototypes. Further design development and material exploration yielded a product that few could resist touching. A reinterpreted textile made from rubber bands taps into people's natural tendencies to seek haptic experiences. In the form of a spatial divider, it embodies the initial goal of having people interface with the textile and ultimately one other.

With similar design ambitions as the previous case study, an intervention on a college campus aims to bring people together (UVA Sound Lounge, p. 88). Special holosonic speakers provide directed "sound showers" that combine with video projection to allow for shared audio and audio-visual experiences within a common area of one of the university's buildings. This ability gives students and faculty the opportunity to plug into the environment as though they were using a communal set of headphones rather than isolate themselves through the use of personal devices. Ceiling and floor conditions, as well as furniture, are designed in service of this feature, reinforcing the designers' social intent.

Designing for sensory stimulation can take many forms, and the range of desired outcomes spans from inward restoration for individuals to outward social interaction among groups of people. Moreover, sensory thresholds provide a means to navigate between levels and types of stimulation, producing a sense of spatial contrast and diversity. An overarching intention of these strategies is to create objects and environments that enhance user experiences and strengthen engagement within the physical realm. Despite significant technological advancements aiding in the design process, the focus of most digital tools used by designers still tends toward enabling visualization. Even virtual reality has its limitations in this regard, requiring multiple peripherals to barely simulate the real qualities of an object or space as experienced through one's full sensory perception. Beyond the design process, there is another technology-driven issue that is perplexing and invading all aspects of life. Personal digital devices seem to lure many away from being present and aware of their surroundings; so, while they may allow people around the world—or just in the next room—to connect in ways that were previously unimaginable, this comes at the expense of interpersonal and environmental connection within a physical place. Therefore, the strategies presented in this chapter offer tactical considerations for designers seeking to reestablish an awareness of people and space in a way that incentivizes communal and immersive experiences with the potential to contribute to occupants' overall emotional and physical well-being.

THE MAGIC THRESHOLD

PHYSICAL AND SYMBOLIC TRANSITION THAT REFRESHES TRAVELERS WITH MIST AND LIGHT
2011

International air travel can incite a flood of emotions as one leaves a country and enters another, often depleting the traveler emotionally and physically. People in transit at Milan Malpensa, however, may experience a brief moment of respite from their journey as they pass through an unexpected space along the route from the airport terminal to the railroad station. The room, which appears more like a void, features a central luminous blade of light creating what the designers refer to as "The Magic Threshold." This transitional space that seemingly lacks a program is intended to give travelers the impression of crossing through a literal and metaphorical gateway, which symbolically may serve as a point of arrival for some and a marker of departure for others. The mesmerizing curtain-like effect materializes as light refracts through intermittent gusts of mist, which can be seen and felt as one moves through it. A field of blue LEDs placed in the floor is reminiscent of runway lights. In the background, monochromatic finishes and low ambient lighting de-emphasize the room's perimeter, making it appear boundless. This interior space possesses the ability to create a heightened sense of spatial and bodily awareness, prompting travelers and other occupants to break from their habituated state of mind.

LOCATION: MILAN, ITALY
DESIGNERS: PIERLUIGI NICOLIN (WWW.STUDIONICOLIN.COM), SONIA CALZONI (WWW.CALZONIARCHITETTI.IT), GIUSEPPE MARINONI (WWW.STUDIOMARINONI.COM), GIULIANA DI GREGORIO
MAJOR PROJECT PARTNER OR COLLABORATOR: ALBERTO GARUTTI (ARTIST)

The pavilion stands in contrast to the surrounding airport context. Visible from above is a skylight that brings in natural light to supplement artificial lighting on the interior.

The concept was inspired by an ancient Roman building technique of placing a pool directly under an opening in the roof to produce a cooling effect by catching rainwater.

Two rows of LEDs installed at the height of 5 m (16 ft) generate a strip of light on the floor measuring 20 m (66 ft) long and 70 cm (28 in) wide, while an integrated nebulizer emits bursts of mist.

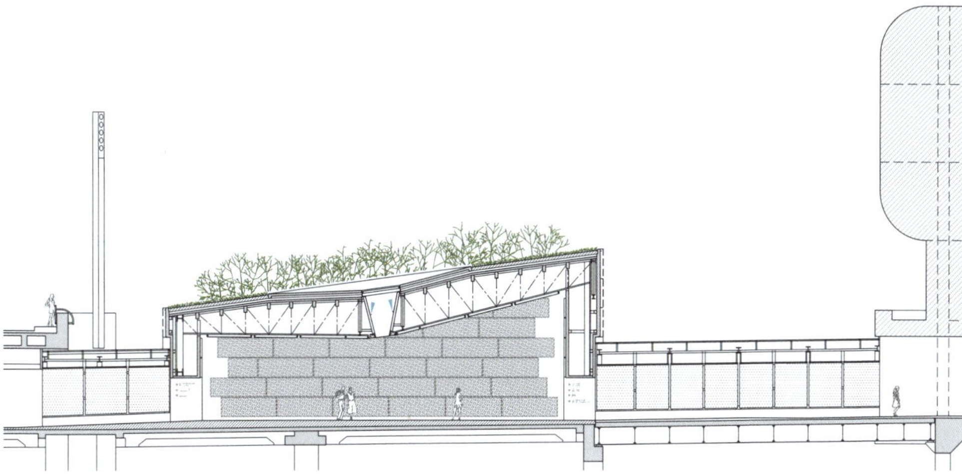

The "Gateway to Milan" is a 900 m² (9,688 ft²) pavilion positioned along a major thoroughfare connecting the airport terminal to the railway station.

A nondescript corridor leads to the installation, heightening the contrast between the spaces. An artist's inscription in the floor reads, "Every step I have taken in my life has led me here, now."

SILENCE ROOM

QUIET SPACE THAT RESTORES SHOPPERS
BY REMOVING SENSORY STIMULI
2013

Department stores thrive on sensory overload, which can be physically exciting but also taxing for customers. The concept of a Silence Room as relief from the overstimulation caused by retail environments was first conceived by Harry Gordon Selfridge, who opened the revolutionary namesake department store in 1909. He was a firm believer in creating shopping experiences that go beyond simply making purchases. Following this spirit, present-day Selfridges launched "No Noise," a marketing initiative that focused on peace and tranquility. The campaign introduced de-branded merchandise, created a series of events focused on meditation, and led to an interior space inspired by the historic Silence Room. The restorative qualities of the quiet space were designed to be in direct contrast to the highly-stimulating surrounding context. The designers aimed to lessen the environmental load on shoppers by removing visual and acoustic noise to the greatest extent possible. The restricted level of sensory information created an atmosphere where people could mentally and physically relax and reenergize before returning to the bustling department store and the streets of London.

Dark, maze-like corridors with plush carpeting acted as a buffer and connected the busy retail area to the inner Silence Room. Soft linear lighting helped guide the way to the destination.

Upon entry, shoppers were asked to leave shoes, cell phones, and other 21st century distractions in the cubbies and lockers provided.

LOCATION: LONDON, UNITED KINGDOM
DESIGNER: ALEX COCHRANE ARCHITECTS (WWW.ALEXCOCHRANE.COM)
MAJOR PROJECT PARTNERS OR COLLABORATORS: SELFRIDGES, EMERALD HOUSE (CONSTRUCTION), GABRIELLE SHAW COMMUNICATIONS (MARKETING)

Muted materials and soft lighting kept the overall visual complexity to a minimum. Overhead mechanical and electrical services were left exposed but masked in a single color.

The felt-clad room comprised of insulated, paneled walls had no functional program other than to serve as a place of refuge and contemplation.

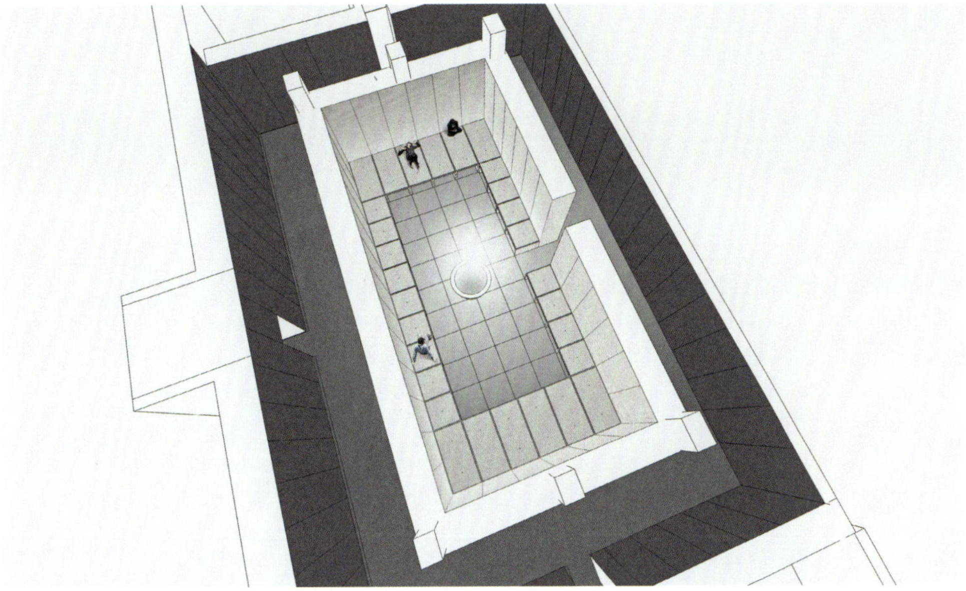

The room-within-a-room was designed on a strict grid and positioned on the lower ground floor of the Oxford Street store near the elevators, a busy walkway, and a restaurant.

Built-in benches afforded visitors a place to sit, meditate, or sleep.

SHADE

RESPONSIVE WINDOW TREATMENT THAT PROVIDES
INTERIORS WITH THE UNPLANNED CHARACTER OF OUTDOORS
2010

Interior spaces often play a passive role, lying dormant and waiting to be activated. The dominant forces within a room are typically the occupants themselves. However, outside of the built environment, weather is a significant factor. The concept of indoor weather is seemingly an oxymoron, primarily since the provision for shelter has evolved through modernization to include consistent interior conditions devoid of the fluctuations found outside. In the search for comfort, people have come to occupy spaces that are static and whose only connection with the outdoors may be a window to the world beyond. In urban spaces, this may only serve to bring in daylight, without even offering the benefit of natural views. Shade, however, is an artwork that seeks

The resulting shadow play was projected onto the floor and walls in the *Hyperlinks* exhibit at the Art Institute of Chicago. The material was programmed to react to measurements taken by an outdoor wind sensor.

A film applied to the surface of the glass consisted of a grid of triangular cells that responsively changed from transparent, to translucent, to opaque.

to bring the outside in through "augmented natural light." It consists of a film applied to glass which is controlled by a combination of software and sensors that detect wind on the exterior and process this information to trigger a response. As a result, the glass appears to have varying degrees of opacity, filtering daylight into an ever-changing play of light and shadow. Over the course of the day, the overall atmospheric effect within the interior continuously shifts and evolves with the movement of the sun. The random and unpredictable qualities

A temporary installation of the film to the oculus of the Victoria and Albert Museum's newest extension expands the concept of Shade from a distinct geometric pattern to an overall ambient condition.

are based on live exterior conditions. Interestingly, purely computer-animated effects do not seem to satisfy in the same way as when people believe the natural world is responsible, which is possibly due to an innate desire in humans to connect with nature. Beyond the pleasure derived from viewing this in a gallery setting, the implications are far-reaching and could alter the way one conceives of interior spaces and their power to heighten awareness of physical space and its relationship to the ecosystem.

Naturally fluctuating exterior conditions filtered through the 7 m (23 ft) high glass facade of the NOW Gallery in London created a dynamic kaleidoscope effect on the interior.

LOCATIONS: LONDON, UNITED KINGDOM AND CHICAGO, IL, UNITED STATES
DESIGNER: SIMON HEIJDENS (WWW.SIMONHEIJDENS.COM)

The wind, as well as the angle and intensity of the sun, were responsible for the effortlessly engaging changes to the interior atmosphere of the V&A Sainsbury Gallery.

The interior of the gallery took on the unplanned qualities often experienced in nature, providing a restorative space for visitors to relax.

LIQUIDROM IN TEMPODROM

POOL THAT INVITES VISITORS TO FLOAT WHILE
LISTENING TO AN UNDERWATER CONCERT
2002

Wellness spas tend to be relaxing and introspective by design. Visual complexity is not the norm, and often interior volumes are kept simple with finishes that are textured and muted in color. Water, in its many forms, is a fundamental element in the creation of spas and baths, taking the shape of pools, showers, and saunas. The Liquidrom is no exception; but here, it is the combination of water and sound that offers a surprising sensory experience. Located within a larger complex that features two stages for public events and performances, the pool at the center of the wellness spa unexpectantly becomes the third stage. As visitors move beyond the minimally designed interior spaces of the spa, they encounter a large, centralized saltwater basin. With a delayed entry sequence, the pool reveals itself slowly, and one notices muffled sounds that are melodic but not distinguishable. It is not until bathers are submerged that they understand that the unclear sounds are, in fact, harmonious underwater. This concept of "liquid sound" relies on a computer-controlled system of speakers above and below the water that functions in conjunction with lighting for corresponding visual effects. Sound waves move faster through water than air, making it difficult to identify their source and giving bathers the impression of being fully immersed in the acoustic experience, which induces a deep sense of relaxation. At times, only a few guests enjoy the soothing qualities, while at others, up to 50 people come together to hear a DJ's mix or a live concert, introducing a new social dimension to what is often conceived of as a contemplative practice today.

LOCATION: BERLIN, GERMANY
DESIGNERS: GMP/ARCHITEKTEN VON GERKAN, MARG UND PARTNER (WWW.GMP-ARCHITEKTEN.COM), MICKY REMANN (WWW.WWW.MICKYREMANN.COM)
MAJOR PROJECT PARTNERS OR COLLABORATORS: MEINHARD VON GERKAN, HUBERT NIENHOFF, STEPHAN SCHÜTZ, WILFRIED SCHOO, MATTHIAS WIEGELMANN, ULRIKE BRUTTLOFF, NICOLAS POMRÄNKE, PATRICK PFLEIDERER, AND JOHANNES ERDMANN OF GMP (ARCHITECTURE); MICKY REMANN (LIQUID SOUND/MULTIMEDIA ART)

Forming a public square, the iconic concrete structure of the more extensive urban complex is home to indoor and outdoor music and sporting events. At its core is a wellness spa concealing a more intimate experience.

The wellness spa covers 1,360 m² (14,639 ft²) and consists of several saunas, steam baths, a hot water open-air pool, a bar and restaurant, and a large saltwater pool as the main feature.

The basin is 13 m (43 ft) in diameter and characterized by a dramatic vaulted ceiling consisting of a domed concrete shell with a central oculus. It contains body-temperature water with a 3% salt content.

Users ascend into the water via steps to make their way toward the pool, which appears from behind a stone-clad wall. Upon entry, musical sounds are out of tune, adding to the other-worldly feeling of the space.

Bathers float on their backs with the assistance of foam supports so that their heads are partially submerged with ears underwater and eyes looking upward to the light display.

Once in position, the magical moment occurs when it is apparent that the indistinct sounds above water are clear and in sync underwater.

ON TENSION

ROOM DIVIDER THAT ENCOURAGES INTERACTION AND TOUCH
2011

Textile design is typically not driven by the question of how it can encourage people to meet and interact with one another, but that was precisely the design objective of On Tension. Given the inherent tactile qualities of textiles, they offer a suitable medium to activate the sense of touch and can thereby influence behavior. The designer began by creating early studies of a flexible surface with the aim to stimulate social interaction, but she observed that people were hesitant to explore the materials initially selected. She then transitioned to low-tech elastic bands to produce the unconventional textile, which is a material that is intrinsically conducive to haptic exploration. It is nearly impossible to hold a rubber band without unconsciously stretching and reshaping it. The bands are held in tension and can be rearranged and connected with magnets, thus providing the physical and emotive properties for an interactive screen. The textile is mounted on a rigid substructure to serve as a partition for dividing rooms into smaller, more intimate spaces. The screen elicits an intuitive response that allows the idea of play to enter into everyday settings. As an unexpected responsive surface, it can be enjoyed by an individual or it may spontaneously spark an interaction among several people. In an increasingly automated and touchless society, textiles can respond to the desire for more material experiences, while also inciting physical contact with objects, spaces, and people.

LOCATION: LONDON, UNITED KINGDOM
DESIGNER: EVA MALSCHAERT
MAJOR PROJECT PARTNER OR COLLABORATOR: ROYAL COLLEGE OF ART

The designer selected elastic bands because of their responsiveness. They were hand-dyed to achieve the desired gradients of color.

The soft, pliable material and enticing colors work in tandem to encourage users to explore the divider in a playful, unstructured manner.

The bands connect with small magnets that can be linked together.

The resiliency of the bands allows them to be changed continually, exhibiting web-like arrangements and different color combinations, which can then be returned to their original state.

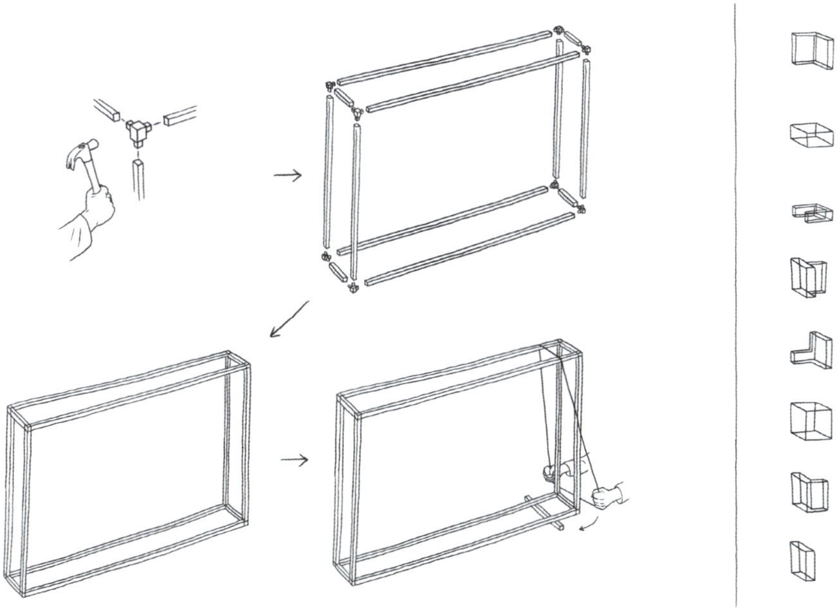

The concept is intended to be installed in a variety of configurations, adapting to a range of architectural conditions.

UVA SOUND LOUNGE

COLLEGIATE STUDENT LOUNGE THAT BRINGS PEOPLE TOGETHER THROUGH SHARED SOUND SPACES
2009

Most public interiors have audio systems that indiscriminately fill the space, subjecting everyone to the same music or television station. A place's soundscape is rarely conceived of holistically alongside its physical design. Now, with the development and popularity of personal devices such as portable media players and smart phones, it is not uncommon for people to drown out their surroundings by listening to music, podcasts, or watching videos, while simultaneously detaching themselves from those around them. The designers approached the renovation of an underutilized university student lounge by employing technology to encourage engagement under a "communal headphone." They conceived of an interactive public realm where sound creates the perception of defined zones within one large open space. In the Sound Lounge, ultrasonic loudspeakers direct a beam of sound within several designated areas, beyond which it is virtually inaudible. These areas are made visible by suspended overhead forms and corresponding floor patterns. Soft, moveable furniture within each of the three zones afford small groups the opportunity to sit under collective "sound showers" and enjoy a shared listening experience, sparking dialogue and communication rather than isolation.

Within the 185 m² (2,000 ft²) lobby, students and faculty can connect personal devices to docking stations to customize their own shared media micro-environments.

The "sound shower" zone ranges from 1 to 3.7 m (3 to 12 ft) across and is visually demarcated on the floor by ovals of coordinating colored carpet.

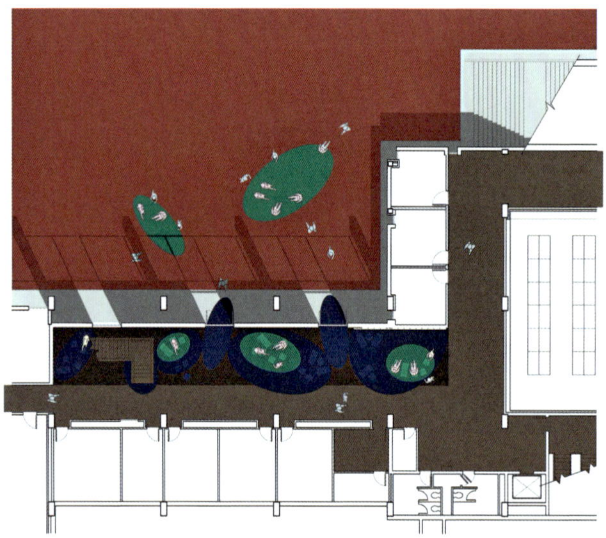

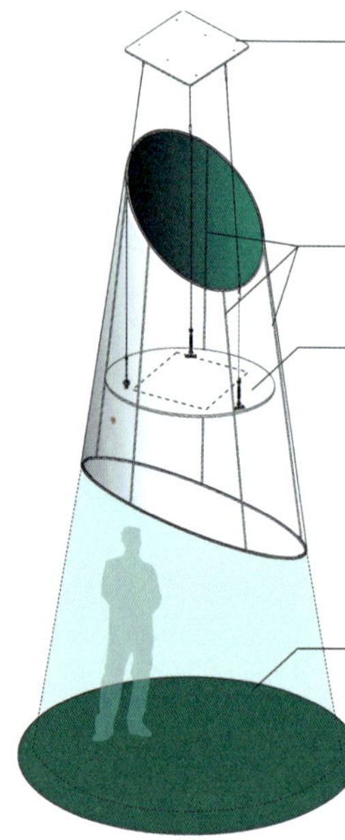

Holosonic speakers, housed within metal frames with stretched fabric covers, project sound directionally so that the output is only audible within a precisely defined area.

LOCATION: CHARLOTTESVILLE, VA, UNITED STATES
DESIGNERS: JOEL SANDERS ARCHITECT (WWW.JOELSANDERSARCHITECT.COM), KAREN VAN LENGEN ARCHITECT
MAJOR PROJECT PARTNERS OR COLLABORATORS: UNIVERSITY OF VIRGINIA SCHOOL OF ARCHITECTURE, LAWRENCE PHILBRICK OF ACENTECH (ACOUSTICS), ARONSON FLOOR COVERING

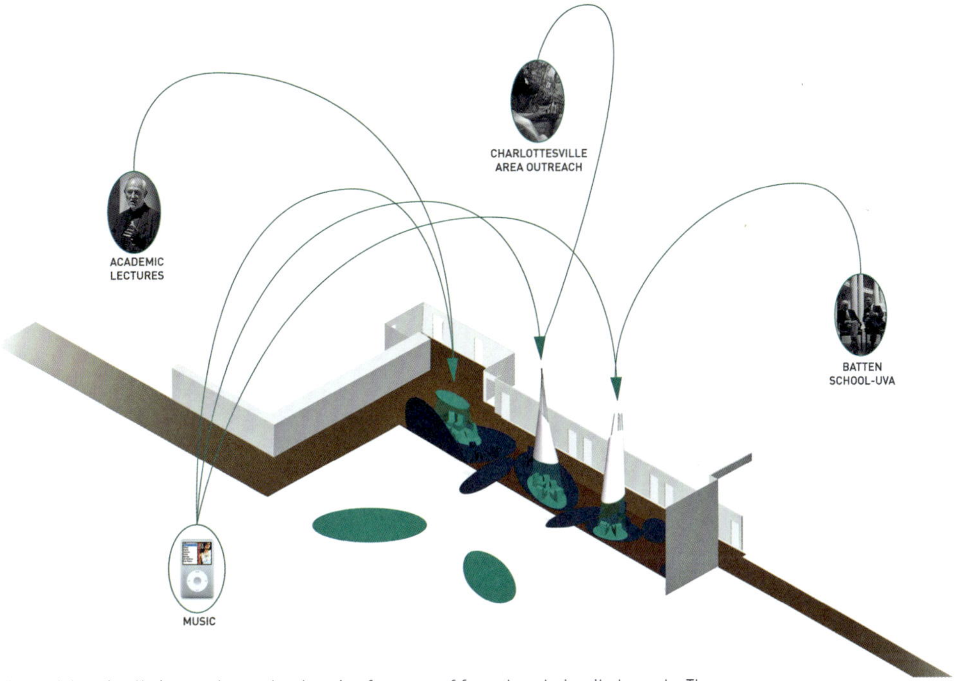

Users determine their soundscape by choosing from one of four closed-circuit channels. The first channel enables them to share their personal playlists, while the other three channels connect to campus, community, or global programs.

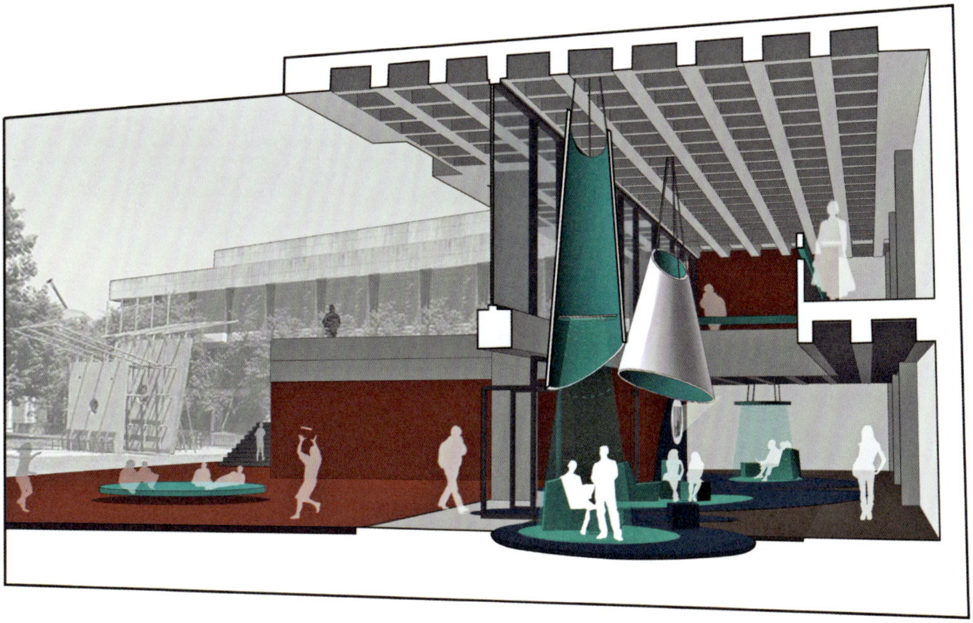

Elliptical-shaped cones suspended from the gridded concrete ceiling take advantage of the double-height space.

The largest area provides a collective audio-visual experience with projected imagery for broadcasting real-time lectures and events from around campus and beyond.

CHAPTER 3

HARMONIOUS INTEGRATION

DEFINITION: A state of physical, psychological, and social congruity between a person and an object or environment; synomorphy

The built environments that people occupy on a daily basis are constellations. Each one consists of a set of spaces, occupied during a certain timeframe, filled with particular arrangements of furnishings and objects. These come together to form behavior settings that support and evoke standing patterns of behavior, which will likely persist even when the participants change. In this sense, many environments are not dependent on the unique differences of individuals. For example, the occupants in a classroom may come and go throughout the day or year, but regardless of the instructor or students, the room is used in more or less the same way each time with only a small range of variability. Overall, when there is similarity between the physical systems (e.g., classroom layout) and the behavioral patterns (e.g., teaching and learning styles) that overlay onto one another within a setting, the resulting positive fit is referred to as synomorphy. This theory is fundamentally familiar to designers because it is most often what one strives to accomplish when creating an object or space.

During the ideation process, designers typically endeavor to read and comprehend how a project's physical, psychological, and social aspects integrate with one another. Without deviating into the mindset of architectural determinism, it is conceivable that one can encourage a certain behavior by altering the behavior setting. Through this approach, it is possible to go beyond the basic accommodation of an occupant and their activities to create a high degree of space-fit. The two design strategies discussed below describe how to achieve a synomorphic state by either perceptively framing small-scale situations or specially tailoring entire large-scale spatial constellations. Thus, the case studies in this chapter exhibit what is feasible when designers possess keen observation skills and an understanding of behavioral research and use these to identify and respond to specific needs within an environment.

STRATEGY: SITUATIONAL FRAMING

Situations define how people meet the world, and they influence individual and group conceptions and behaviors as they learn how to deal with them. More precisely, a situation is a combination of circumstances, or the aggregate of biological, psychological, and sociocultural factors that surround an individual or a group and that condition their behavior patterns. Notably, the word situation also refers to being located or positioned within an environment, so it is not void of physicality. Therefore, situated, place-based behaviors can become starting points for designers of both products and spaces. It is the appropriate framing of beliefs, ideas, and relationships that surround a situation that leads to synomorphy. Some situations are generic, while others are idiosyncratic, but each reveals unique opportunities for supporting the respective activities taking place. The following serve as examples of what can result when one takes a closer look at a particular situation and allows the design solution to grow out of this analysis.

Every day, in offices across the globe, people gather around ubiquitous tables for meetings where they discuss, brainstorm, and strategize. To date, the study of proxemics has provided guidelines, such as what constitutes competitive and noncompetitive seating arrangements, and the conveniences of integrated power and WiFi access have become expected norms. However, on the whole, very little has changed when it comes to the act or situation of holding a meeting. People scramble to take notes with the aim of capturing the topics discussed for reference later. The process of documenting a meeting can be cumbersome and even inhibiting to the goal that brought everyone together in the first place. Hence, the design of one table seeks to do more (Listening Table, p. 100). Through the table's synthesis of industrial design and software development, it is a piece of furniture that enables. It listens, records, interprets, and even forgets over time so that meeting participants can go about more important business matters.

Situational framing has also proven useful for a more unusual environment, one that many people may never experience firsthand. In prisons, inmates who suffer from mental health and other well-being issues are often underserved. It can be challenging to transport them to the necessary healthcare providers, and within the facility, there is often a lack of suitable space to render this type of care. One designer's identification and study of this situation became the impetus for the development of a mobile pod, which can be located as needed within an institution's walls (seedS, p. 104). The complex conditions of the prison environment led to a customized intervention that takes into account the place-specific needs related to safety, comfort, and privacy of both the prisoner and the therapist. Not surprisingly, since these units meet the stringent requirements of the original context for which they were designed, they are now also used for a variety of other purposes.

Moving on to a retail situation, the process of selecting a paint color is one that excites and bewilders many customers. For instance, who knew there were so many whites? The designers of one retail display system looked to behavioral research that explains the phenomenon that occurs when people with too many choices experience difficulties making decisions (ColorSnap Studio, p. 108). By understanding people's tendencies and behaviors, designers can reconsider how to address a set of circumstances to better support the task at hand. This new system introduces steps into the selection process to narrow and streamline choices, reducing indecision and the time it takes to select a color from over 1,000 options.

STRATEGY: SPATIAL TAILORING

Spatial tailoring expands outward from the micro-level of a single situation to the macro-level of an entire network of situations, with the intention of fashioning spatial ecologies that better address needs and leverage opportunities. Indeed, this strategy summarizes the daily practice of many designers who spend their time thoughtfully shaping spaces, furnishings, and objects. To achieve congruity between people and their surrounding environment, the designer must first discover the underlying similarities between the physical structure of a place and how people experience it. Moreover, while it may be helpful information at times, the concern is not with which one causes the other. Since structure and experience cannot be isolated, the aim is to understand the set of relationships that exist between the complex systems at work and then design for their harmonious integration or fit. The following examples showcase how this strategy can yield highly adapted and customized spaces and products that respond to human-centered programmatic needs and desires.

Designing workplaces is a complex challenge. They become physical manifestations of company culture, employee working styles, and individual differences. Adding to the difficulty, many new companies, especially in the tech industry, experience volatility that results in scrappy office designs. This has become such a signature characteristic that even established companies want to embody the "start-up" ethos, complete with a highly flexible work environment and an anti-corporate aesthetic. The designer of one workplace furniture system spent time in Silicon Valley observing people in their settings and witnessing their ad-hoc ways of furnishing their office spaces (Hack, p. 110). This ethnographic approach resulted in product features for the new system that allow for mobility and adaptability with a less refined finish. Large areas of workstations are quickly rearrangeable, and individual employees can adjust their workspace to suit their personal preferences.

Another space experiencing change is at the core of education. The traditional classroom with its rows of desks facing one direction is inherently not conducive to new collaborative and active learning methods or the use of modern technology. An astute assessment of the conventional model, along with extensive design research, observation, and testing led to the keen redesign and, significantly, the reconfiguration of classroom furniture (LearnLab, p. 116). The simple premise of moving the "front" of the classroom to the "center" of the room changes the dynamic of the space entirely. It not only makes better use of the space and its perimeter, but it more effectively supports new teaching techniques that include both digital and analog means.

Nursing homes exist to meet the needs of a select population, yet the standard institutional approach employed by many facilities delivers impersonal medical care and strips residents of their identities. In this final example, an entire neighborhood designed to offer nursing home care to individuals living with severe dementia is decidedly not focused on clinical care but on living life with services when needed (De Hogeweyk, p. 122). Instead of ward-like surroundings, residents live in homes created to reflect their past lives. Details such as art, dishware, and decorations are intentionally selected to lend a sense of familiarity. With the help of family input and a lifestyle assessment tool based on extensive data collection, residents move into homes that will most likely be "socially compatible environments" where they will share similar values with others in the household. The surrounding village context further simulates everyday life with a central boulevard, gardens, and destinations like restaurants and clubrooms that are designed to embody a sense of place and normalcy. On the surface, all looks ordinary, but on closer inspection, subtle differences appear. One of many situational examples is the supermarket. It has rows of recognizable products, fresh produce, and a "cashier," but there are no price labels and employees are trained to interact with individuals living with dementia. This level of integration between the social and behavioral needs and the physical environment is a hallmark of this strategy.

Empathetic programming is at the core of designing for synomorphy. This process involves a close examination of individual situations and entire networks of behaviors, which designers may realize through a range of design research methods and an understanding of evidence-based research. Despite the skill level required, people may easily overlook a designer's contribution to a project that achieves harmonious integration. This oversight often happens because a well-designed space or object that programmatically supports people's needs quietly recedes into the background. Once occupied, there is little regard for the intense effort that went into the design of an accommodating space. Similarly, this effort goes unnoticed with an object in use unless it becomes evident that it has resulted in a poor fit. While the strategies in this chapter are opposed to a one-size-fits-all approach, it would be irresponsible not to address that even the best of intentions resulting in a highly customized solution can still sometimes miss the mark. A design may not function as intended or a user's needs may have changed or evolved since its inception. Designing for people in real-world environments comes with a level of uncertainty and unpredictability. It is helpful to remember that space is not an abstract concept but rather a behavioral phenomenon. It does not necessarily follow the predictions of the designer. Instead, a designer must make informed assumptions, follow these with testing and evaluation, and then embrace the reality that future change and adaptation is inevitable. As such, the built environment and the objects within it are an organic extension of the everyday lives of its inhabitants rather than merely the conception of a sole creator involved in an idealized artistic endeavor.

LISTENING TABLE

MEETING TABLE THAT HEARS, UNDERSTANDS,
AND DOCUMENTS CONVERSATIONS
2014

As a universally accepted signal to gather, even the most basic of tables is inherently an example of social furniture. The Listening Table though goes beyond being a simple prop for social interaction and uses technology with semantic listening abilities to make meetings more effective and engaging. Its streamlined appearance intentionally juxtaposes traditional wood joinery and contemporary materials. The circular shape removes any sense of hierarchy among those seated around it, and the table's enhanced features are physically expressed through their form. Microphones link to an application that transcribes conversations, freeing attendees to participate fully without needing to take notes. With specially developed speech-processing software, the table has interpretive capabilities and recognizes all participants of the meeting as well as the topics of greatest importance. At any time, users may tap one of the many capacitive strips to drop a virtual marker indicating a significant moment. Afterward, a semantic overview outlines the discussion, while digital recordings of the 30 seconds before and after each marker was dropped are extracted. A conventional, mechanical on-off switch shuts down the software for anyone who wants to opt out, and all recordings are erased and forgotten after four weeks.

LOCATION: NEW YORK, NY, UNITED STATES
DESIGNERS: THE NEW YORK TIMES R&D LAB (WWW.NYTLABS.COM), UM PROJECT (WWW.UMPROJECT.COM)
MAJOR PROJECT PARTNERS OR COLLABORATORS: NOAH FEEHAN OF NYTLABS (CONCEPT, SYSTEMS, ELECTRONICS DESIGN/FABRICATION), FRANÇOIS CHAMBARD OF UM PROJECT (INDUSTRIAL DESIGN/FABRICATION)

The table facilitates and augments human interactions by allowing continuous eye contact and the free flow of ideas.

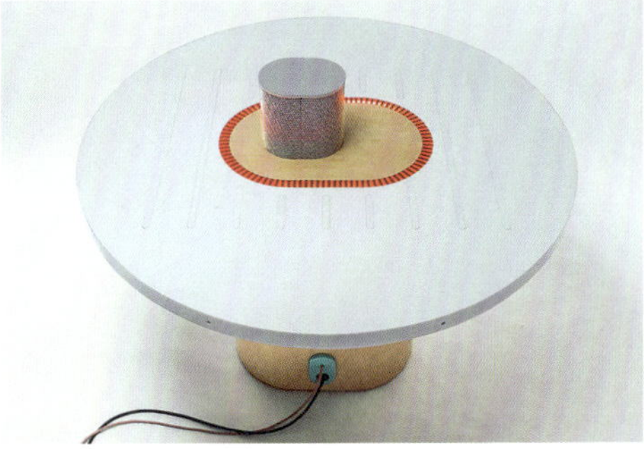

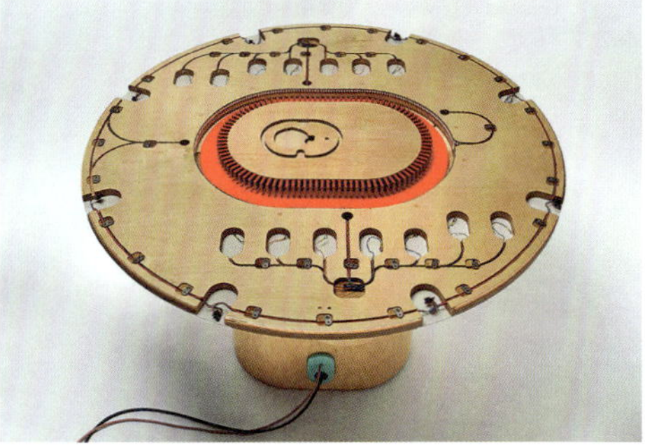

Beneath the surface is a system of software and hardware with simple cabling, none of which connects to the cloud to keep data localized.

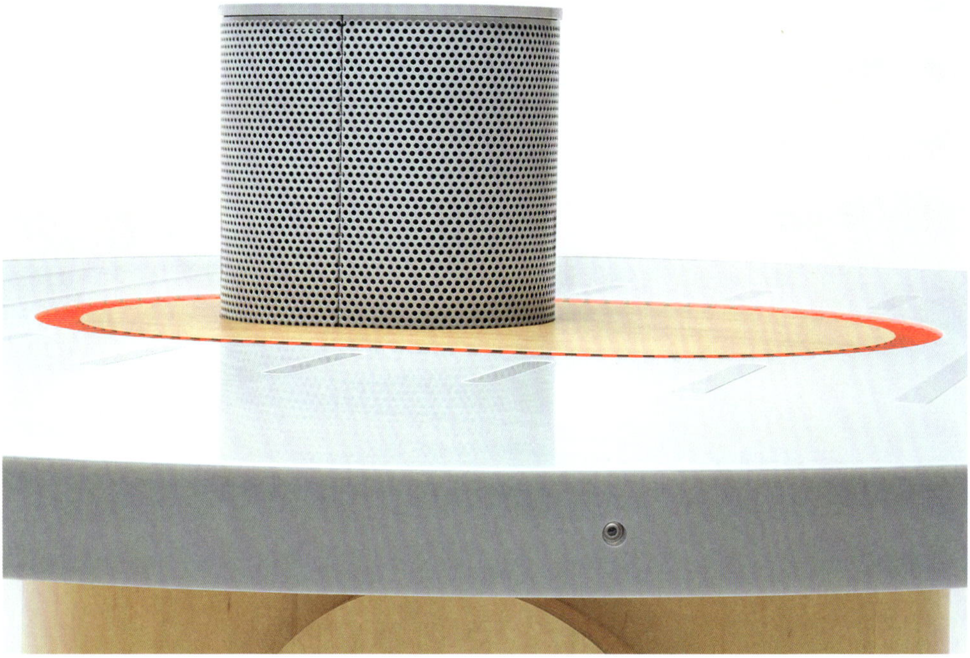

Thermal cameras detect attendees' positions, while a dynamic microphone array captures voices from multiple angles.

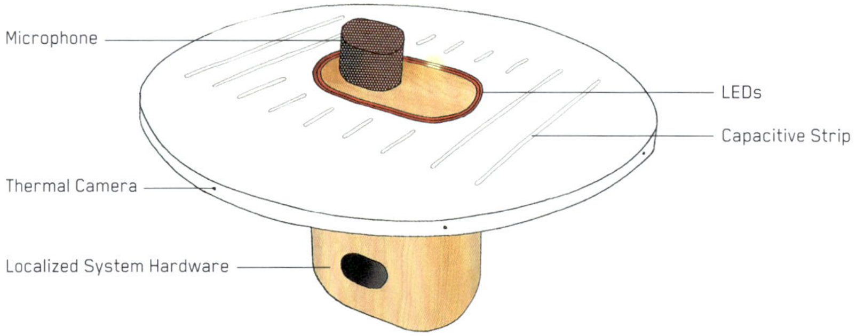

Technological features were designed to be easy-to-use and expressive of their function.

Physical features, such as the on-off switch and pulsating LED lighting that indicates recording is in progress, ensure that the table's purpose is transparent and that people are willing participants.

The table takes notes as a person would, recalling only the broad strokes and defining moments of a meeting rather than every word.

SEEDS

MOBILE THERAPY SPACES THAT GIVE PRISONERS ACCESS TO MENTAL HEALTH SERVICES
2015

Prisons are known to be harsh places, and it can be a challenge to meet all the inmates' needs, especially with issues like overcrowding and staff shortages. Mental health is a subject that is regularly neglected when facing these shortcomings. Disruptive behavior leading to assaults and even death, as well as self-harm and suicide, is not uncommon. Many incarcerated individuals are not only in poor physical condition, but they often suffer from some form of mental illness and could greatly benefit from receiving a range of healthcare services. A significant hindrance to rendering health and well-being services is the lack of suitable clinical space. The designer of seedS responded by creating a free-standing treatment room that can be "planted" directly within prisons. This approach allows a high number of patients to be seen on any given day, with the option for the unit to be relocated wherever services are needed most. The pod-like design embodies human nature's inherent desire for shelter by offering a safe and private micro-environment for inmates to access the therapy that will ultimately aid in their rehabilitation and reintegration into society.

Equipped with a table and adjustable colored lighting and speakers, therapists can control the interior setting, while high-density foam core walls dampen the external sounds of the prison.

The pods can be temporarily placed within an open prison environment and relocated as needed.

The unit is finished inside and out with fiber-reinforced plastic for durability and infection control and features a removable panel that can serve as an emergency exit.

LOCATION: LEEDS, UNITED KINGDOM
DESIGNER: KARL LENTON OF SAFE INNOVATIONS (WWW.SEEDPODS.COM)
MAJOR PROJECT PARTNERS OR COLLABORATORS: LEEDS COMMUNITY HEALTHCARE NHS TRUST, STAGE ONE, THE SIR JOHN CASS SCHOOL OF ART, ARCHITECTURE AND DESIGN, UNIVERSITY OF LEEDS, MINISTRY OF JUSTICE, PRISONERS

Smooth lines and therapeutic sensory features convey a calm atmosphere within a hostile environment.

Safety and security were considerations in creating the interior, which does not have any ligature points to help ensure users do not cause harm to themselves.

The 2.4 m (8 ft) diameter pod comprised of eight modular pieces is assembled in half an hour without screws or clips, which could be misappropriated as weapons.

COLORSNAP STUDIO

DISPLAY THAT REDUCES THE NUMBER OF CHOICES
TO SIMPLIFY PAINT COLOR SELECTION
2015

With thousands of options, selecting a paint color can be an overwhelming task. Most paint companies show their entire color library at once in retail displays, which may be visually attractive but possibly counterproductive. Psychological studies have shown the potentially paralyzing effects of choice overload, which can lead to difficulty in making decisions. The Sherwin-Williams in-store display aims to remedy this by rethinking the paint selection process. Despite adding 200 new colors to their palette, the retail system seeks to expedite the selection process, hence improving the customer experience. ColorSnap Studio uses rotating panels to group colors by family, directing patrons to consider a reduced number of hues such as red, yellow, or blue before proceeding toward more granular selections that are organized by saturation level. This new approach also does away with the familiar narrow strips in favor of larger single-color paint chips. The paint company conducted in-store tests and found that, on average, color choices were made in 60% less time in comparison to their previous display. The physical kiosk was designed as part of an integrated color-selection system that also includes online tools and an expanded professional toolkit.

Paint chips can be scanned using a mobile app to see room scenes rendered in the selected color along with suggested coordinating colors.

Each panel has a single color on one side representing the overarching color family and a palette of approximately 50 corresponding paint chips on the opposite side.

The interactive display features 24 rotating panels and a central work area where customers can arrange and review color selections. New printed color guides and postcards provide additional inspiration.

LOCATION: SHERWIN-WILLIAMS STORES IN THE UNITED STATES AND CANADA (4,000 LOCATIONS)
DESIGNERS: IDEO (WWW.IDEO.COM), SHERWIN-WILLIAMS (WWW.SHERWIN-WILLIAMS.COM)

HACK

WORKSTATIONS THAT PROVIDE FLEXIBILITY FOR CONTINUALLY CHANGING "START-UP" ENVIRONMENTS
2016

"New economy" companies are notorious for their rapid growth and volatility, which coincides with a particular work culture and environment. Start-ups, and even more established tech companies, are characterized by their casual workplaces and unconventional attitudes toward office design. The reason for this is not only their ever-evolving space requirements but also their ethos as creators and innovators who are always iterating and developing new ideas. On a research trip to Silicon Valley, the designer of Hack witnessed firsthand how furniture solutions ordered online and quickly assembled or made locally with off-the-shelf materials were preferred over more sophisticated corporate furniture. This observation of behavior in situ led to a new system that is flexible in use, relocatable, and intentionally understated and informal in appearance. In comparison to other systems, it can more aptly respond to dynamic workplaces and a variety of work modes, while also having a versatile, raw aesthetic that is decidedly uncharacteristic of most commercial office furniture. Fittingly named, "hack" is a technology term that dates back to the 1950s when MIT used it to describe a skillful and resourceful solution.

The unit's flexibility allows for sit-stand workspaces, private booths for lounging or meeting, or an impromptu coffee bar or print station.

The system's unfinished look reflects a cultural attitude toward the workplace as an environment where the only constant is change itself.

LOCATION: BASEL, SWITZERLAND
DESIGNER: KONSTANTIN GRCIC FOR VITRA (WWW.KONSTANTIN-GRCIC.COM)
MAJOR PROJECT PARTNER OR COLLABORATOR: VITRA (MANUFACTURING)

The three-sided unit provides for individual preferences by having a flat surface that adjusts for standing or sitting without impacting neighboring workstations or the sightline across the office.

The units have large hinges so they can be collapsed for new layouts or storage.

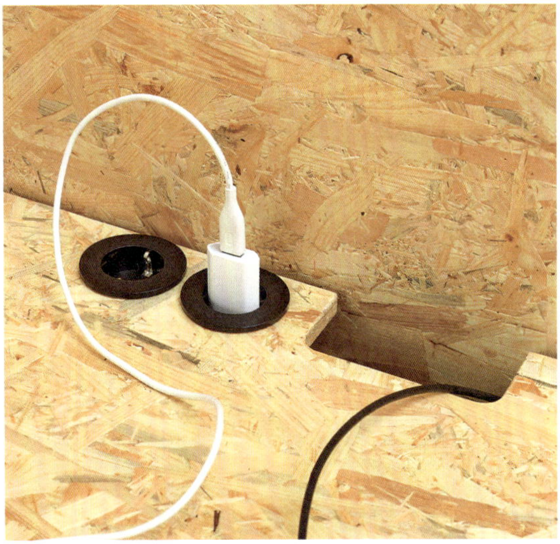

Constructed from oriented strand board (OSB) with practical electrical and cable management components, the units are easy to rearrange without special tools or worries of damaging the finish.

A manually operated hand crank raises and lowers the surface from 30 to 125 cm (12 to 49 in).

The high sides of the units provide booth-like privacy when used as seating.

LEARNLAB

CLASSROOM THAT SHIFTS THE FRONT OF THE ROOM
TO MULTIPLE STAGES FOR INTERACTIVE LEARNING
2007

Currently, a transition is taking place in the work environment that prioritizes "learning workers" over "knowledge workers." In the process, the need for higher education to adapt becomes even more critical. While technology is now the great enabler, the conventional physical classroom has become more of a barrier. Based on user-centered research and extensive observation, Steelcase developed the LearnLab, an environment that promotes active learning. A room's shape and furniture arrangement have a significant impact on its social dynamic. The LearnLab reconsiders the geometry of a typical room and how information can be triangulated throughout the space rather than focused toward the front. Without a front or back to the classroom, students have equal access to content and improved sightlines, while the instructor can interact and move about more freely. Vertical surfaces and corners are used for multiple types of display from projection to whiteboards and monitors, which allows content to remain accessible throughout the class for better retention. The LearnLab oscillates between single- and multi-focus modes facilitating different ways of sharing information. It is a promising example of what is possible when technology, furniture, and the built environment are thoughtfully integrated.

LOCATION: GRAND RAPIDS, MI, UNITED STATES
DESIGNER: STEELCASE EDUCATION (WWW.STEELCASE.COM)
MAJOR PROJECT PARTNER OR COLLABORATOR: STEELCASE'S WORKSPACE FUTURES (RESEARCH)

Most classrooms still have a hierarchical layout of rows of front-facing desks oriented toward a blackboard and lectern.

A square floor plan with a centered door makes use of the room's corners, while positioning furniture in an "x" configuration removes the room's sense of hierarchy.

Monitors are placed in corners for better viewing, while walls support removable "huddleboards"—whiteboards hung on tracks. Swivel chairs permit students to pivot and orient themselves as needed.

Annual Property Claims

The spatial arrangement allows for smooth transitions between multiple teaching and learning styles without breaking cognitive flow.

Team-based collaborative work can be displayed and shared easily with the rest of the class via low- and high-tech means.

Students can move from receiving information, to discussing it, and then communicating it to others.

DE HOGEWEYK

VILLAGE THAT SUPPORTS PEOPLE LIVING WITH SEVERE DEMENTIA
2010

What began as an experimental ward in a nursing home outside of Amsterdam in the 1990s has evolved into a purpose-built "weyk," an old Dutch word for neighborhood. Inspired by the type of care the founders would want for their loved ones, it is more than a physical place. It is a complete cultural shift from the care people living with dementia typically receive. These individuals experience stress in a variety of situations and often lose their sense of time and place. Thus, a traditional nursing home usually only adds to their confusion. This may lead to behavioral disturbances and increased medication, which can speed up an individual's decline and decrease their quality of life. De Hogeweyk, which receives the same government funding as other facilities, moves away from a medical system toward a social relational system. Instead of an institutional setting, the physical surroundings support daily activities and interactions that closely simulate everyday life. Residents live in houses with all of the components of a family home, and the designs reflect a range of "lifestyles" recalling commonly shared values and cultural backgrounds. Here, residents are treated as equal participants in their care and given autonomy to make choices. Free to come and go as they please within the village, patterns of normal living for residents revolve around household decisions, such as planning for the day's meals, chores, and activities. Together with staff, they regularly go on outings to the village supermarket, and at other times they may visit the theater or hairdresser, or stop in at the café. De Hogeweyk reports positive effects of "small-scale living" for its residents, including better cognitive and functional capacity, reduced aggression, and improved social engagement. Nonresidents are also welcome to enjoy the neighborhood amenities where they can be seen mingling with residents and staff who all wear plain clothes, lending a further sense of life-as-usual in this extraordinary place.

A total of 152 residents with severe dementia live in houses accommodating six to seven individuals, supported by a team of staff. The exterior facades safeguard residents from the world beyond.

LOCATION: WEESP, NETHERLANDS
DESIGNER: VIVIUM CARE GROUP (WWW.BETHECARECONCEPT.COM)
MAJOR PROJECT PARTNERS OR COLLABORATORS: VIVIUM CARE GROUP (FOUNDER/INTEGRAL CONCEPT/INTERIOR DESIGN), MOLENAAR&BOL&VANDILLEN ARCHITEKTEN (ARCHITECTURE), NIEK ROOZEN BV (LANDSCAPE ARCHITECTURE)

The property covers a city block and contains 23 houses with 17 designs, totaling 15,310 m² (164,800 ft²). Similar to a traditional Dutch village, houses line the perimeter and orient toward a central square and gardens.

One main secure point of entry and exit allows residents to move independently throughout the village without concern that they may find themselves on the outside.

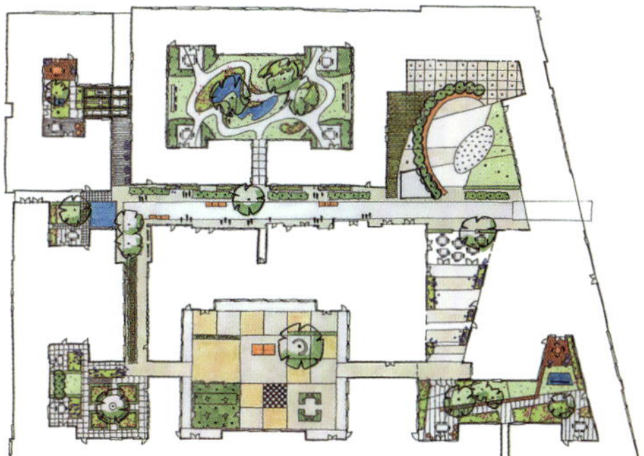

Buildings cover half of the property, and the other half is outdoor space. The integrated exterior and interior design helps residents understand and navigate their surroundings.

House designs reflect four Dutch "lifestyles" expressed through their interior design and décor. Each has a different floor plan, materials, colors, and furnishings.

Staff play a role akin to a family member supporting someone in their own household. The focus is on living, well-being, and care as they go about normal daily activities, such as preparing meals, shopping, and laundry.

Amenities such as a supermarket, salon, theater, pub, and more are designed to be recognizable. There are also many clubs, events, and outings that create a vibrant society.

CHAPTER **4**

INTERACTIVE TRANSACTION

DEFINITION: An informative action or activity involving a person and an object or environment that reciprocally affects or influences each other

Designed spaces and objects can affect users, just as users can affect designed spaces and objects. This is explained by transactional theory, which focuses on relationship patterns and the notion that humans and the environments they occupy are mutually supportive. As a construct, it is in direct opposition to the perspective offered by separatism in which people and the environment are separate entities, with one dominating over the other. It is true that people often shape their environments to serve their needs, wielding their power over them, but reciprocal relationships between people and the built environment are becoming more prevalent. In this chapter, low-tech and ad hoc examples are presented alongside projects featuring sophisticated technological advancements. At the pinnacle of this category are artificial intelligence and ambient technology, which make it possible for behavior learning and sensing features to be embedded seamlessly into products and the built environment, enhancing their responsiveness to people. The case studies below and the strategies they represent overlap and progressively build in intensity. The first strategy proposes forming unconventional alliances that casually connect individuals and objects to one another. Fully immersive partnerships, on the other hand, raise the level of exchange between occupants and the built environment to promote a higher degree of interdependence among them.

STRATEGY: UNCONVENTIONAL ALLIANCE

Most objects and spaces are designed to meet a particular goal, but perhaps not as explicitly as the examples in this chapter. While many projects begin with setting aspirations, some go further to create designed objects and spaces that are active companions, assisting a person to achieve a specific purpose. This approach leads to an unexpected bond between people and the inanimate where each has a pronounced influence on the other. In this way, the user does not dominate over the object or environment nor does the design dictate the user's behavior. They must ultimately work together in an alliance where neither takes a passive position. Dynamic actions often involving motion, touch, or sound are inherent to creating an interactive transaction. At times, a movement or activity of the user triggers a single response—a light turns on, or a chair seat lowers—while at other times it sets off a complex series of ongoing interactions where the designed object or space responds to an individual in a continuous loop of action and reaction.

It is not uncommon to think of furniture as supporting various forms of social interaction. Sociopetal and sociofugal furniture arrangements, for example, either group people so that they may communicate directly with one another or position them away from one another to discourage eye contact and maintain privacy. In these instances, the placement and orientation of seating supports the desired outcome, but it is somewhat ancillary to the social interactions that take place, acting as more of a prop than a prompt. What if an object's ability to promote activities or interactions were less latent? Through the case study of a light fixture whose ability to function is reliant on people's behavior (Social and Anti-Social Lights, p. 134), it is possible to understand how this object also supports introverted and extroverted interactions, but in a more dynamic, responsive way.

Spaces and furnishings more often than not fulfill general needs, but when they are part of an integrated constellation working in tandem with technology, they can help users form a stronger connection with their surroundings. People have begun to treat their mobile devices and wearables as prostheses to their bodies, but this type of relationship does not exist to the same extent between people and their physical environments. Another point of view is to regard a person and their near environment, inclusive of furniture and other close-range objects, as a holistic entity. A chair (Clūnēs, p. 136), for example, in conjunction with tracking technology can encourage its owner to become more active by offering a visual signal, reminding the user and those around them of a daily fitness goal one hopes to achieve.

Furthermore, entire environments can become part of a synergistic approach to address the needs of a person. In the case of compact living, it is often necessary for the occupant to coordinate their desired behavior within the limited setting. For space saving reasons, all programmatic functions cannot be present at once, which forces the user to activate their environment as needed. In one unique example that is notably not dependent on technology, this idea is taken to the extreme, requiring the tenant and their living quarters to engage in a lockstep union to realize living in a small footprint (Roll-it, p. 140).

STRATEGY: IMMERSIVE PARTNERSHIP

Embedded smart technology and the Internet of Things (IoT) are dramatically changing products and by extension inhabitable environments. The merging of the digital and physical worlds is presenting new possibilities at a rapid speed, requiring an even greater level of integration in the design and implementation process. Some of the most insightful and inspiring examples are found in the coalescence of technology and the built environment, which also take into account behavioral and evidence-based research. Immersive surfaces that create a sensorial engagement give way to artificial and ultimately ambient intelligence that allows three-dimensional environments to be sensitive and responsive to the presence of people and even learn from their behaviors. The more sophisticated the network becomes, the more the technology begins to blend into the background to become an always-on digital atmospheric layer that is in sync with its occupants' physiological and psychological states. It is here, where environments begin to respond to people's behaviors and even emotions, that immersive partnerships take hold.

People of all ages have grown accustomed to interactive touch screens, and it is a seemingly natural transition that this technology scales up to become a full-body interaction incorporated into constructed spaces. In this case study, a relatively unremarkable corridor comes to life and exhibits a playful attitude (Cabrini Hospital Malvern Art Installation, p. 146). The programmable system is capable of producing effects in response to an occupant's movement and touch, as well as various environmental factors such as the weather, time of day, or the number of people present. In a hospital, personal devices can provide positive distractions and opportunities to connect with others. However, a large interior surface with no visible computer hardware or screens may be less obtrusive and friendlier toward in-person social interaction.

Considering a different set of circumstances, there are special populations, such as children with autism, that often find themselves in socially isolating situations. The advanced haptic technology of a playscape aspires to an even more complex set of ambitions than the previous examples in this chapter (Social Sensory Architectures, p. 152). This project involves providing pressure-sensitive feedback to children with special needs while offering them social opportunities. A technologically-enhanced knitted surface yields the necessary resistive material quality to activate a series of physical and visual rewards, and it can also be stretched into a three-dimensional form for an encompassing spatial experience.

For centuries, people have acclimated themselves to spaces, from the interiors of caves to the contemporary buildings of today. However, now, it is possible for spaces to adjust to inhabitants and not merely the other way around. A series of pods, each with different interiors conducive to stress reduction, is capable of adapting to provide personalized experiences (RESET, p. 156). Conditions within each microenvironment respond to the user's heart rate and brain activity until reaching an optimum mental state. Biofeedback obtained through monitoring devices is offered to the occupant so they can make real-time adjustments in situ, presenting the occasion for environment and occupant to harmonize. This level of integration leads to paradoxical experiences. At first, the responsive space encourages occupants to become hyper-aware of their surroundings, especially as the environment reacts to their presence, movements, and even preferences. As this association becomes symbiotic, the environment may seemingly withdraw, allowing the occupant's attention to drift as the technology's situational awareness becomes more attuned.

Interactive transactions center on relationships. They generate connections between users and their surroundings, often with a view toward sociability. With these strategies, designers will leverage new technology and find innovative low-tech approaches to create products and spaces that are increasingly able to assist with accomplishing daily activities and achieving goals and aspirations. Sometimes this will be for the pure enjoyment of it, and other times the design will have far more elaborate aims. In its most advanced state, the concept of conceiving of spatial conditions as a series of transactions offers opportunities for the built world to become a humanlike companion or for individuals to physically plug into a programmable digital network. A reoccurring theme appears throughout this chapter, which is a cautionary one. There is an innate desire for people to feel present in the physical world while also enjoying all the benefits of technology, suggesting that the key going forward will be finding the right balance between the two.

SOCIAL AND ANTI-SOCIAL LIGHTS

LIGHT FIXTURE THAT EITHER NEEDS TO BE SPOKEN TO OR LEFT IN SILENCE TO FUNCTION
2001

Pendant lights, like most other furnishings and fixtures within interior spaces, are typically subservient to the occupant. Lighting is there to be turned on and off, provide illumination, and at times, fulfill a decorative role. The Social and Anti-Social Lights may appear unexceptional, but they were developed to react to their environment. Featured in the Walker Art Center exhibit "Strangely Familiar: Design and Everyday Life," each one forms a social interdependence with the inhabitants of the shared space. Designed to be responsive, it is up to the occupant to prompt the desired effect through their behavior, entering into a relationship with the fixture. The Social Light is activated when it detects sounds such as people talking. It may, for example, be used to

The Anti-Social Light will only provide illumination if complete silence surrounds it. Any noise will cause it to wane and switch off.

The Social Light needs to be the center of attention. It will only stay lit if encircled by the sounds of activity and conversation.

reinforce social exchange around a dining table. In contrast, the Anti-Social Light requires absolute quiet to function. Voices, ambient sounds, or other noises cause the light to dim until it turns off. It is only actuated by silence, providing light for reading or other introspective activities. Bringing inanimate objects to life by requiring them to be less submissive and more companion-like could potentially alter our association with products, how we interact with others, and ultimately how we create spaces.

LOCATION: MINNEAPOLIS, MN, UNITED STATES
DESIGNER: STUDIO MICHAEL ANASTASSIADES (WWW.STUDIOMICHAELANASTASSIADES.COM)
MAJOR PROJECT PARTNER OR COLLABORATOR: WALKER ART CENTER

CLŪNĒS

CHAIR THAT RAISES ITS SEAT REMINDING SEDENTARY WORKERS TO BE MORE ACTIVE
2015

Many people rely on smart phones and wearables to track their movements with the aim of becoming more physically fit, but the fascination with such devices can quickly fade. In developing future products focused on healthy living for IKEA, one of the world's largest furniture manufacturers, the designers of this prototype observed a missing link between wearables and the surrounding physical context. They also endeavored to reduce the reliance that people have on screens and instead imbue common objects with behavioral cues to offer positive encouragement. They began to explore how physical artifacts can nonverbally communicate and decided on chairs because they inherently express sedentary behavior. This speculative concept imagined for workplaces, or other types of environments, helps the user externalize their health ambitions to those around them who may, in turn, provide moral support. Clūnēs is a product that suggests that traditionally static furniture pieces can become dynamic companions in everyday life and part of a greater motivational network.

Clūnēs works in conjunction with an existing digital app that has an integrated motion tracking chip that records users' activity data such as steps and distance traveled.

Unlike traditional chairs, which are motionless, Clūnēs reflects the state of the user's daily health goal. If it is unmet, the seating surface is elevated.

LOCATION: COPENHAGEN, DENMARK
DESIGNERS: MELINA PYYKKÖNEN (WWW.MELINAPYYKKONEN.COM), LILIANA LAMBRIEV (WWW.LILIANALAMBRIEV.COM)
MAJOR PROJECT PARTNERS OR COLLABORATORS: IKEA AND SPACE10 (CLIENT), COPENHAGEN INSTITUTE OF INTERACTION DESIGN

A swiping motion across the capacitive sensor in the wooden seat resets the chair.

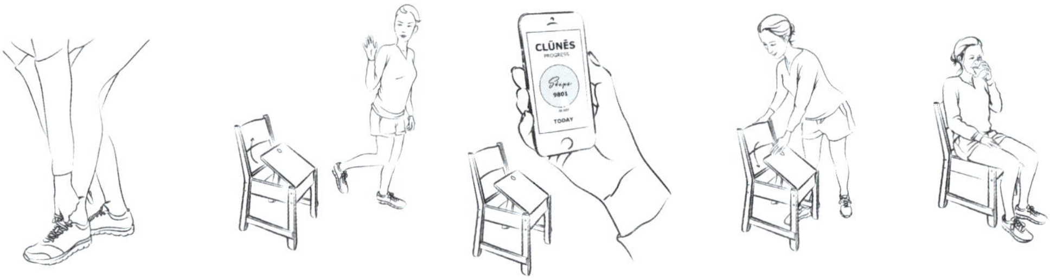

Smart technology is paired with a familiar object, allowing it to exhibit responsive behavior with the aim of promoting an active lifestyle.

The prototype is an existing chair retrofitted with a motor and sensing technology.

ROLL-IT

HOUSING UNIT THAT MOVES WITH THE INHABITANT
2009

The lack of housing in university towns in Germany provided the impetus for a student competition to design a "Guerilla-Home." The brief called for a mobile dwelling unit that could be assembled overnight in open public areas and then quickly be disassembled and moved away once authorities discovered it. Roll-it, the winning entry, is a working prototype reminiscent of a barrel. Within a minimal volume, the students maximized surface area by conceiving of micro-living in the round. Three revolving sections, which must be continually rotated and repositioned, integrate all essential living functions. The apartment is always in motion, both within the interior and on the exterior, as it moves from place to place, requiring active engagement from the occupant to achieve the desired arrangement. While the experimental design presents a new set of challenges, it calls into question the static quality of more conventional spaces that serve as passive backdrops to living rather than forging dynamic relationships with inhabitants. Here, a union forms where the user and built environment mutually influence and affect one another.

The cylindrical components include a living section with a bed and table surface, an exercise section with an area for walking and running, and a plumbed section for kitchenette and bathroom functions.

The program required that the nomadic unit be easily transportable via a trailer.

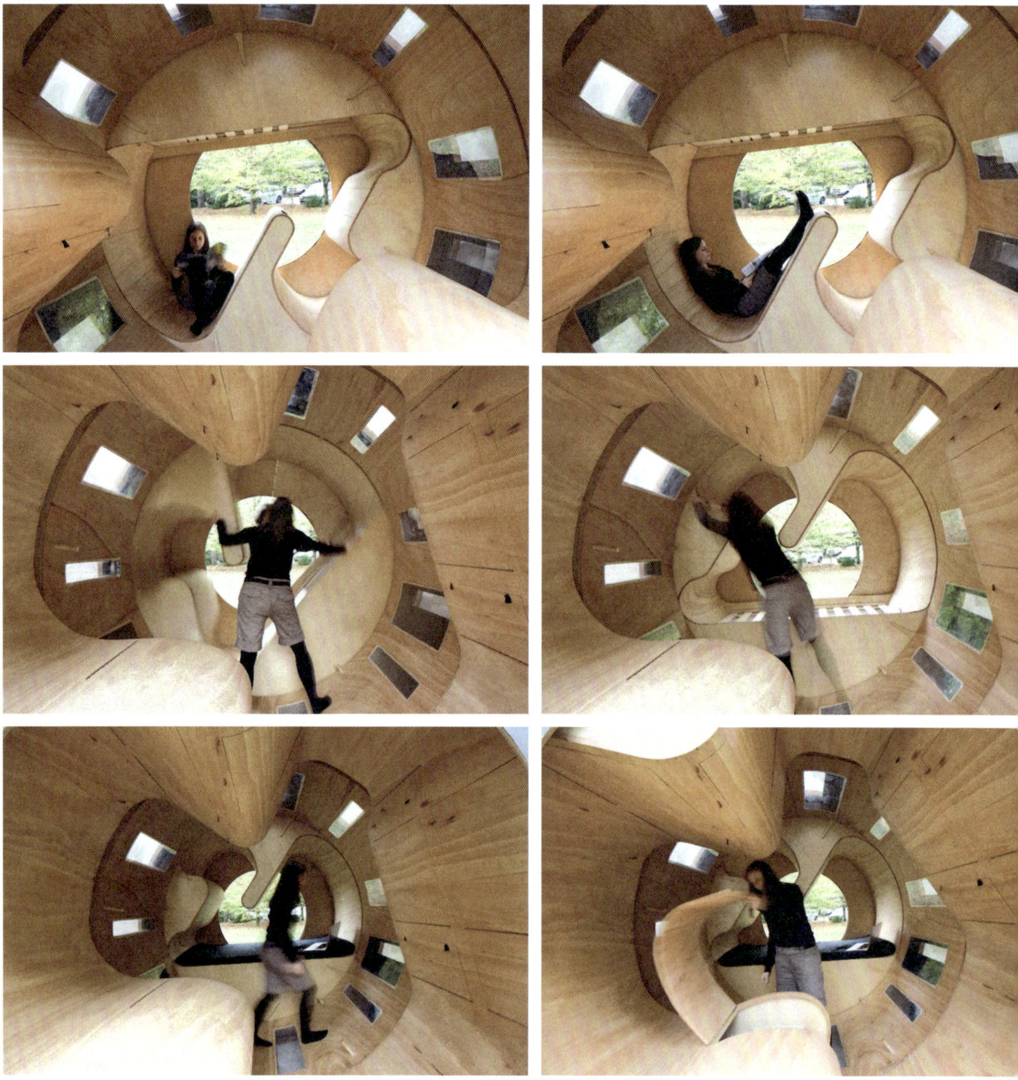

Three revolving sections can be arranged by the occupant according to need. The integrated furnishings and fixtures not in use roll overhead.

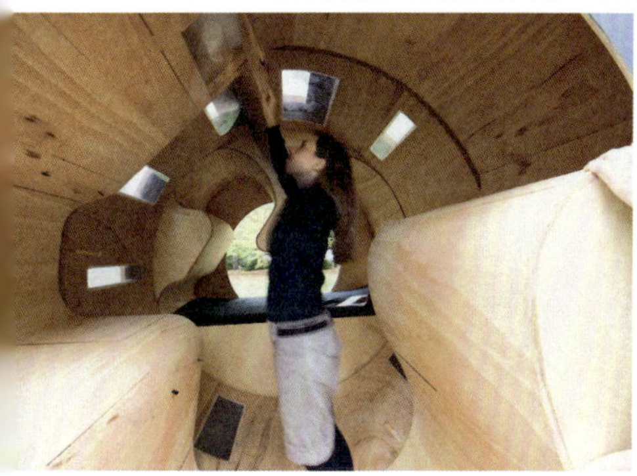

LOCATION: KARLSRUHE, GERMANY
DESIGNERS: CHRISTIAN HEIGL NÉE ZWICK, AND KONSTANTIN JERABEK (ORIGINAL CONCEPT)
MAJOR PROJECT PARTNERS OR COLLABORATORS: BIRGIT BRAUN, JOHANNES FLAMM, SIMON FOTO, MATTHIAS HÖFKER, CORDULA HOERNER, MARIANNE PREISSLER, SEBASTIAN SALOPIATA, VASILIKI SOFOKLEOUS, CAROLIN STEMPFLE, MONICA UDREA, CHRISTIAN HEIGL NÉE ZWICK (DESIGN AND CONSTRUCTION); DIPL.-ING. FH CAMILLE HOFFMANN, DIPL.-ING. MATTHIAS MICHEL (SUPERVISING ENGINEERS); KARLSRUHE INSTITUTE OF TECHNOLOGY

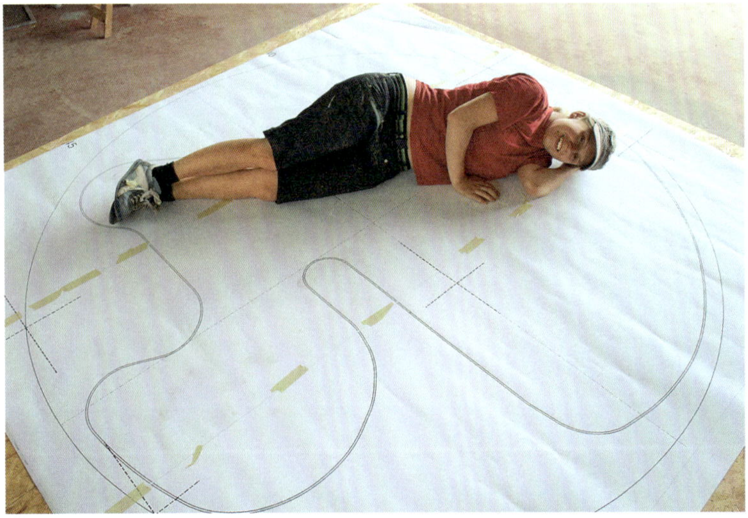

The interior is efficiently designed to be ergonomically and functionally supportive.

The compact 7 m² (75 ft²) mobile unit is intended for temporary placement in open areas such as parks or parking lots.

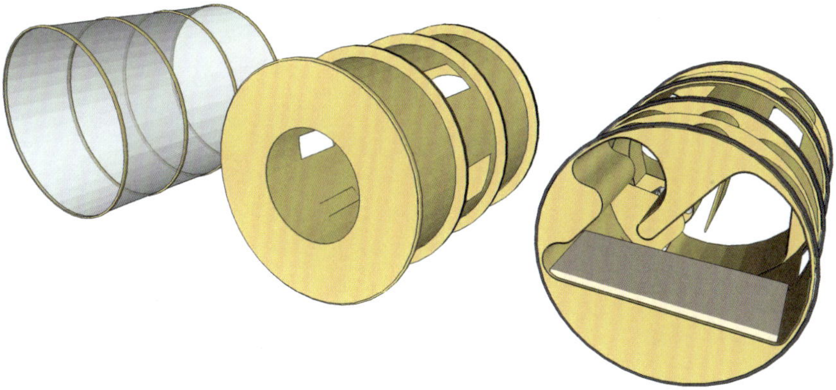

Four structural rings each hold an inner and outer shell, allowing the interior components to rotate independently from one another and the exterior. A waterproofing membrane protects the unit.

CABRINI HOSPITAL MALVERN ART INSTALLATION

CORRIDOR THAT RESPONDS TO ITS SURROUNDINGS AND PASSERSBY
2016

Located in a pediatric ward is an interactive art installation under the guise of a typical hospital corridor. A series of light-emitting panels clad in wood veneer blend inconspicuously into their surroundings. The LED array springs to life when activated, revealing a series of playful scenes. Intentionally absent are projectors or monitors in favor of a solution that integrates fully into the built environment. A driving inspiration for the designers was the opportunity to create a positive distraction in the form of animations with the aim of reducing anxiety in young patients. The use of wood offers an alternative tactile experience to digital screens while also having other attributes such as a visible grain that is known to possess restorative qualities. Programmable software controls the pixelated light display, allowing for generative and interactive content that bestows this interior surface with the ability to react to touch as well as movements, weather, time, audio, and a range of other environmental conditions. Passersby momentarily become captivated through their interaction with the built environment, which in turn recognizes their presence.

Comprised of twelve wood veneer covered LED panels and three acrylic panels, measuring 175 x 50 cm (68 x 19.6 in) each, the installation blends seamlessly into the corridor.

The activated scenes include such features as birds that perch on the handrail, growing grasses, raindrops that fall and splash on people, and airplanes that fly overhead.

The animation is triggered by passersby as it responds to their varying speeds, heights, and movements. As people approach, images become larger.

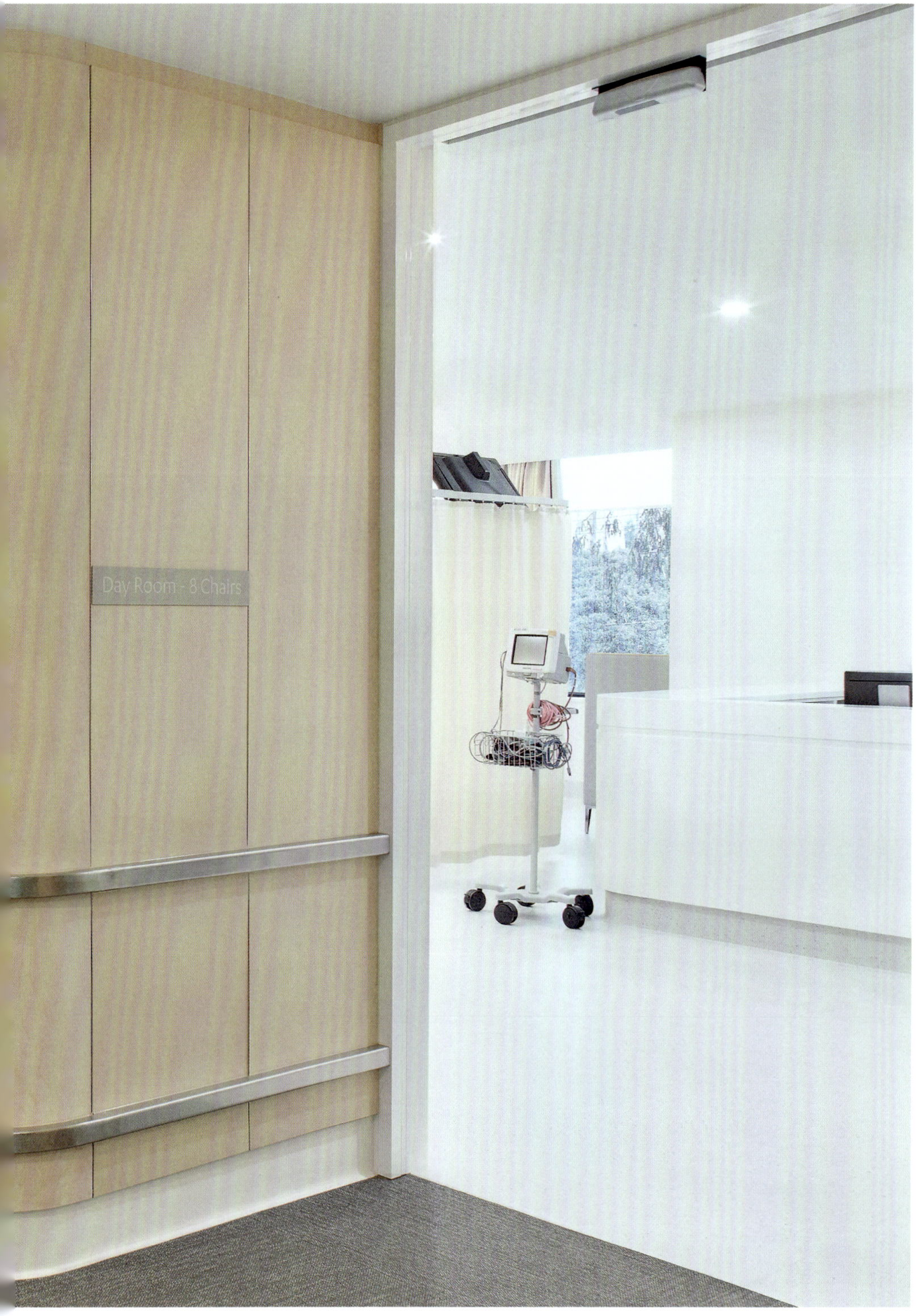
Day Room - 8 Chairs

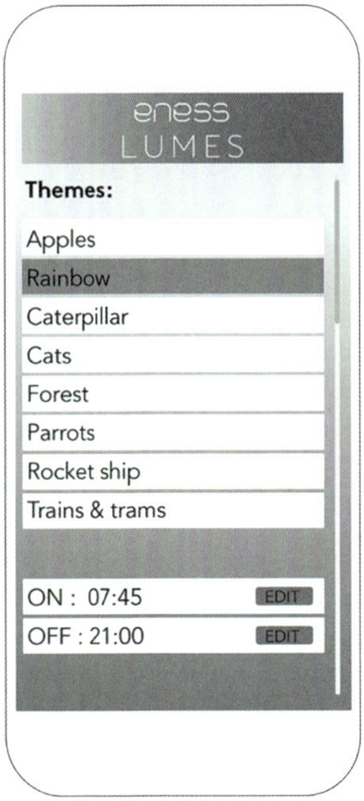

The client can set themes and operation times through a custom app. Once installed, the content can be refreshed and updated remotely.

LOCATION: MELBOURNE, AUSTRALIA
DESIGNER: ENESS (WWW.LUMES.NET)
MAJOR PROJECT PARTNERS OR COLLABORATORS: DESIGNINC (ARCHITECTURE), CABRINI HOSPITAL MALVERN (CLIENT)

The panels can adapt the size of a pattern and its intensity of color and light based on human touch and applied pressure.

The visuals can be programmed to correspond to a variety of environmental conditions such as time of day, outside temperature, or overall activity levels.

SOCIAL SENSORY ARCHITECTURES

PLAYSCAPE THAT PROVIDES SENSORY FEEDBACK
AND ENCOURAGES SOCIAL INTEGRATION
2015

Children with autism often exhibit impairments in the development of fundamental fine and gross motor skills and a deficit in the ability to process sensory information. Regardless of a child's cognitive capacity, these physical limitations can significantly impact how well they assimilate with others socially. This prototype aims to provide a vehicle for combining sensory engagement with motor-based tasks to positively reinforce social play. The tensile structure encourages interaction at multiple scales, ranging from the hand as it engages with the tactile surface, to the body as it moves through the micro-environment. Custom software with tracking capabilities augments the playscape with projected animations. Movement and contact activate the responsive assembly offering tactile, visual, and acoustic rewards. The haptic quality of interacting with the knitted surface differs from

An earlier two-dimensional prototype with a life-size projection of a coloring book graphic demonstrates the user interface. The amount of pressure applied to the surface dictates the "painted" color.

The fluid form is made possible by stretching computer numerically controlled (CNC) knitted textiles within a flexible, glass-fiber reinforced framework.

that of a touch screen, which is critical to someone with autism, who may have difficulty accurately gauging the appropriate degree of pressure. Dynamic digital imagery and sound effects are materially entwined with the flexible mesh, providing a feedback loop based on intensity, duration, and location of contact. This network of features allows children to individually and collectively hone their motor and social skills.

LOCATION: ANN ARBOR, MI, UNITED STATES
DESIGNER: SEAN AHLQUIST (WWW.MATERIALARCHITECTURES.COM)
MAJOR PROJECT PARTNERS OR COLLABORATORS: UNIVERSITY OF MICHIGAN TAUBMAN COLLEGE OF ARCHITECTURE AND URBAN PLANNING AND MCUBED RESEARCH GRANT (SPONSORSHIP); COSTANZA COLOMBI, RESEARCH ASSISTANT PROFESSOR, U-M DEPARTMENT OF PSYCHIATRY; LEAH KETCHESON, POST-DOCTORAL STUDENT, U-M SCHOOL OF KINESIOLOGY; DALE ULRICH, PROFESSOR, U-M SCHOOL OF KINESIOLOGY; OLIVER POPADICH, GRADUATE STUDENT, U-M TAUBMAN COLLEGE OF ARCHITECTURE AND URBAN PLANNING

Interaction with the surface manipulates the movement of projected swarming objects, such as a school of fish. Sustained pressure generates an attraction point that the objects gravitate toward and encircle.

Certain dynamic animations are only activated by simultaneously touching two trigger points, which at times are too far apart for one person and require coordination with others.

In addition to engaging with the responsive animations and sound projections, children enjoy occupying the tent-like structure, which yields a fully immersive experience.

While stimulating in many applications, the elastic textile surfaces and tunnels can also have a comforting quality for autistic children, who often seek out snug spaces.

RESET

SPACE THAT ADAPTS TO REDUCE STRESS LEVELS
2017

Work-related stress is thought to lead to burnout and poor mental and physical well-being, which in turn impacts individuals' quality of life as well as businesses, healthcare systems, and the economy. RESET (Responsive Emotional Transformation) was conceived to combat this issue by providing stress reduction using a variety of scientifically proven methods. A working prototype installed at "Work 3.0—A Joyful Sense of Work" at the Salone del Mobile in Milan demonstrated how the modular pods could be inserted into workplaces, or other environments, to provide useful information via active and passive immersive experiences. The aims of this fully integrated approach are two-fold. Firstly, it recognizes that people respond to stress reduction methods differently. For example, some welcome meditation while others may need to blow off steam. People are encouraged to learn what method works best for them using their personal "RESET Index," an algorithmically derived score and set of recommendations based on their encounters with different types of pods. Secondly, a network of sensors and wearables allows users to receive real-time feedback. Atmospheric conditions within the pods, such as lighting and sound, correspond to the data providing personalized environmental cues to help users reach their desired state of stress reduction.

LOCATION: MILAN, ITALY
DESIGNERS: UNSTUDIO (WWW.UNSTUDIO.COM), SCAPE (WWW.CREATESCAPES.COM)
MAJOR PROJECT PARTNERS OR COLLABORATORS: BEN VAN BERKEL WITH TINA KORTMANN, WILLIAM DE BOER, JESSE ZWEERS, MARCO CONTE, GARY POLK, YANG LI, SANDER VERSLUIS, ERGIN BIRINCI, OANA NITUICA, AND MACHTELD KORS OF UNSTUDIO (ARCHITECTURE); JEFF POVLO, NICOLA TORDOFF SÖHNE, CHRIS MALBON, AND STEVEN SMITH OF SCAPE (SOCIAL DESIGN); DR. TERESA DE SANCTIS (NEUROSCIENCE/EXPERIENCE DESIGN AND OPTIMIZATION); JURJEN SÖHNE (TECHNOLOGY INTEGRATION); DIEDERIK VEELO, RIO KIERKELS, ALVIN GOH, COEN SPOOR, MACHIEL BANEN, BENJAMIN BOURGONJE, AND PAUL SLUIMERS (TECHNOLOGY/INTERACTION DESIGN)

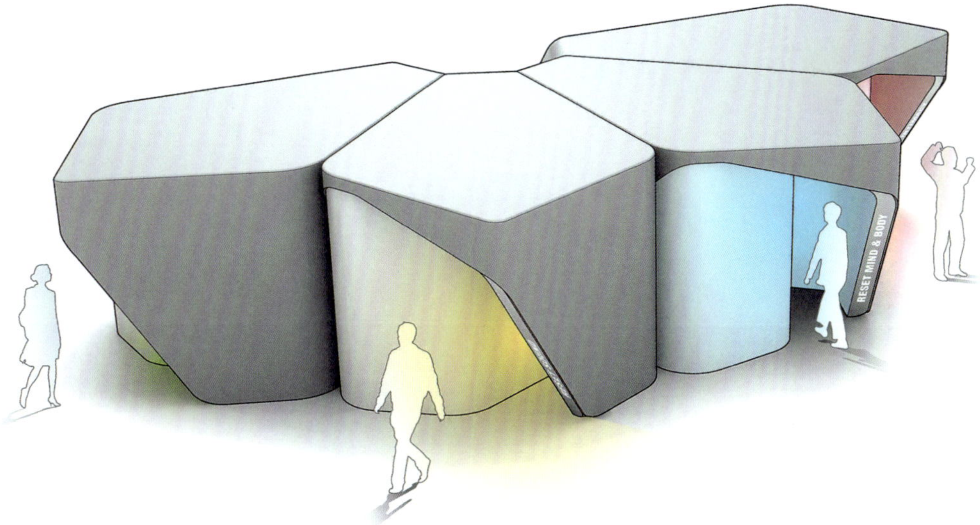

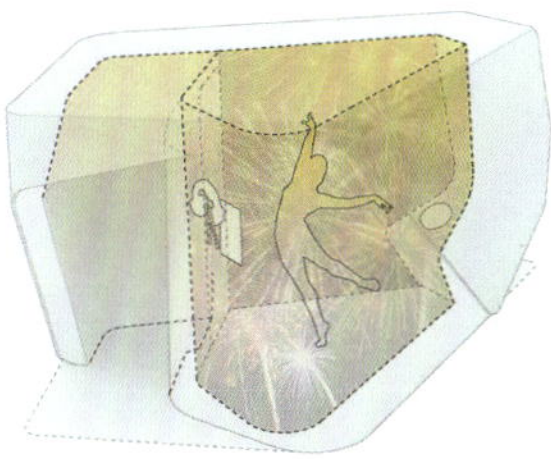

Sound

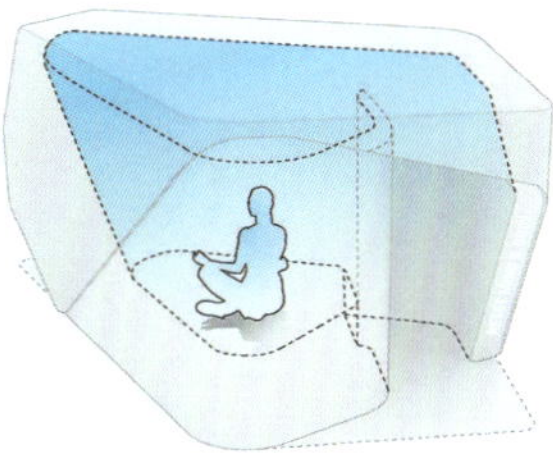

Mind & Body

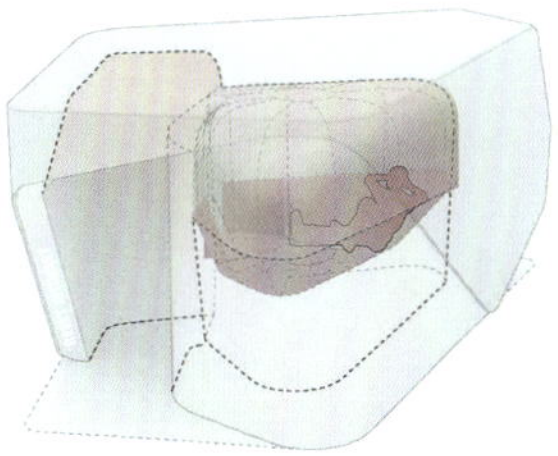

Intimacy

The deployable, modular structures form a cluster of up to six pods. Each unit's interior is designed to relate to the human body and the radius of the experiential activity it supports.

Depending on the type of experience contained within the pod—Intimacy, Mind & Body, Escape, Fight or Flight, Sound Therapy, or Laughter—the entry threshold may offer either a gradual or an abrupt transition.

Wearing wireless headphones in the Sound Therapy pod, occupants jam on electric drums and interact with the surfaces to discover sounds. The light display responds to increased activity.

An elevated heart rate enlivens the space through pulsating lights and ambient sounds that slow along with the occupant's heart to reinforce a meditative state.

Visitors remove their shoes upon entering the Intimacy pod and sit or lie down within the womb-like environment intended to promote feelings of security similar to a warm embrace.

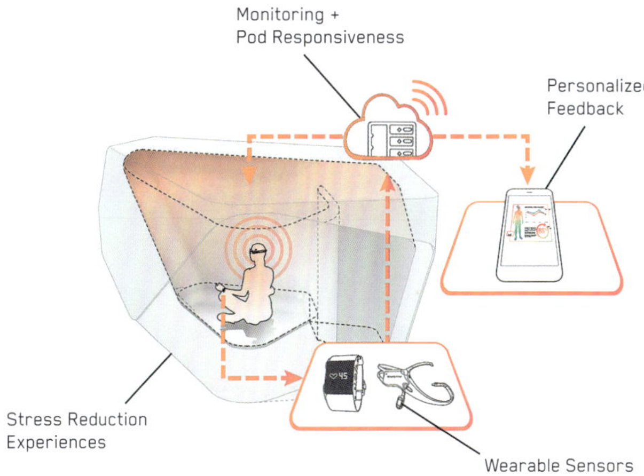

Biofeedback assists individuals in determining how to reduce stress effectively. Data collection is linked to sensors within the micro-environments to provide uniquely tailored user experiences.

CHAPTER **5**

SPATIAL TRANSFORMATION

DEFINITION: The act or process of changing an object or environment in form, appearance, nature, or character; requiring user participation or action

People shape the built environments around them on a regular basis. These changes span from rearranging the furniture in a room to constructing entirely new cities. Control is a critical underlying aspect in this process as people strive to manipulate their surroundings to fit them. Having control within environments has positive benefits for individuals, while the lack thereof can lead to feelings of frustration and helplessness. Control theories state that there are several types of personal control that people have within the places they occupy. The first is behavioral control over one's actions and the ability to make changes within an environment. Next is cognitive control over the interpretation of events that take place within a space; and finally, there is decisional control through the ability to choose a response from a range of options. This chapter presents examples that illustrate how control in all of these various forms plays a role in spatial transformation. The following case studies are spaces and products that set the stage for the inclusion of users in their performance over time. The first strategy explores the traces that people's actions leave behind in the built environment, which can be anticipated and planned for so that individuals are permitted to leave their mark. The subsequent strategies explore how versatile design features and new technologies enable users to configure or change an object or space themselves.

STRATEGY: BEHAVIORAL TRACES

Environments and products come alive with occupation and use. As people inhabit spaces and utilize objects, they inherently change them, often leaving behind implicit behavioral clues. There is a natural accumulation of belongings within spaces, while surfaces and finishes begin to show wear, sometimes almost immediately. This trace evidence can visualize the behaviors or behavior patterns that occurred in an environment, and it may imply what is likely to happen there later. The conception period of a designed object or space is typically insignificant when compared to its full life cycle, but it can be difficult and sometimes impossible for designers to see past the point of creation and anticipate the future. Human-centered design research methods such as observation and usability testing, along with a general sense of empathy, can reveal invaluable insights. It is also helpful to study how other spaces and objects have changed over time and how these changes are perceived. Are they thought to have become better or worse with occupation and use? This particular strategy requires low or no effort on the part of the user and should release them from worrying about their impact on their surroundings, which is something to be celebrated. The physical and material quality of spaces and objects is undeniable, as is the destructive nature of occupation and use. The key is to embrace the inevitable changes that are beyond one's control as positive attributes and set the expectation that occupants, spaces, and finishes will live and evolve together.

While contemporary art museums tend to be experimental worlds, the concepts in this first example (Tensta Konsthall, p. 166) are inspirational for many other types of applications. It is not shocking when exteriors of buildings and outdoor environments wear and weather, but this is usually far less welcome indoors. Public interior spaces are especially subject to extreme use and its effects can begin to show quickly. Surfaces scratch and furniture can be moved easily. These realities were foreseen in the design of this case study and became its motivation. The idea of attrition and loss was part of the planning process, which influenced the furniture selection and led to the development of living finishes that reveal patterns of use.

In today's fast-moving disposable society, new products are often not cherished as they age and show imperfections. The example of a tablecloth (Underfull, p. 170) contradicts this contemporary attitude and aims to become a lifelong possession. The designer accounted for the textile's degradation over time by considering how the pattern and color will change, and in doing so, also manages to shift users' perceptions. An action like tipping over a wine glass typically causes embarrassment, but here it is transformed into something to be appreciated. The more haphazard the user is, the more unique and genuine the product becomes. The buildup of spills cannot be removed, nor would one want it to be since it adds to the memory and narrative of the piece, making it irreplaceable.

STRATEGY: USER TRANSLATION

Behavioral traces are relatively passive on the part of the user. A more active way to achieve spatial transformation invites participation from others to configure objects and spaces to suit their own needs and desires. A kit-of-parts or modular approach can strategically put a system or framework in place that then requires user input to realize its potential. As seen with employing behavioral traces, the designer must be similarly future-focused to anticipate possible scenarios. Also, prototyping and usability testing can be critical to the project's development to understand how it will most likely be used. An initial need for flexibility or adaptability in a particular setting, for example, may kick-start the design process, but the ultimate goal is to empower people to personalize and customize their experiences by giving them choices. Sparking self-expression and creation passes control from the designer to the user. Notably, it is feasible to reset the projects in this category for the next person or group to take over.

Multifunctional furniture inherently has a way of imparting control to occupants. A reconfigurable modular sofa (Sosia, p. 172) can adapt to multiple spaces as well as to different social situations. What makes this example unique is its ability to transform from an object into a micro-environment. Through this feature, it supports both introverted and extroverted activities, and its easy rearrangement lets the user fluidly navigate between the two states.

Certain circumstances, like the aftermath of a disaster, call for quickly deployable solutions (softshelter, p. 174). In response to the need for temporary accommodations, this collapsible system can partition space and give privacy and control to those in a precarious position. The setup and layout of the spaces are up to the occupants. A series of complementary accessories provide additional opportunities to adapt and personalize the temporary shelter.

At other times, it may be desirable to create a system that does not have preconceived ideas about its use. Despite the fact that playgrounds are intended to promote fun, they often lack creativity by having equipment with predetermined, singular purposes. On the contrary, a playground designed as a series of soft, interlocking components (Imagination Playground, p. 178) can generate endless possibilities, relinquishing all control to the users, in this case, children.

5

STRATEGY: VIRTUAL CONVERSION

Some transformations are not reliant on physical means, but they are no less impactful. It has long been possible for lighting and sound to be employed to change an environment dramatically without constituting a material change. As technology develops, especially augmented reality, the possibilities become even greater. As the name of the strategy implies, physical environments are merged with the virtual world to create a space that is simultaneously tangible and intangible. Given that construction is expensive, time-consuming, and generates a lot of waste, change can be prohibitive. In this context, the ability to construct a blank slate and layer on readily modifiable finishes and elements is appealing. Given a choice, could it be more satisfying to be in a space enhanced by augmented reality that is suited to one's preferences rather than spend time in an entirely physical space that lacks personal appeal?

The transportive quality of mixed reality spaces is impressive, and in the case of one marketing campaign (Welcome Home, p. 184), the use of projection made "travel" to different parts of the world instant. Personalization and customization of physical spaces could soon happen at the push of a button, allowing for immediate changes to be made for the next person. While nothing quite replaces being within a fully realized environment, visual textures and animations can evoke similar emotional affects.

Spatial transformation is about power and control, in the sense that there is a transfer that takes place from the designer to the user. Sometimes the user is powerful in a passive way and at other times quite actively. One might say that designers already anticipate the future through the creation of projects, which is true. There are opportunities though to push the conceptual timeline out further and thoughtfully anticipate how an object or space, or its perception, may be altered. Built-in changes allow for living finishes to evolve, and flexible design features permit settings to be reconfigured according to individual preferences. Furthermore, emerging technology will not only offer new tools for designing and constructing spaces, but it will influence the way we occupy them. Presently, most built environments do not adapt at will, but they may have the ability to in the not too distant future. This new capability raises questions and opportunities for contemplation about what one should construct versus what conceptually can be an ephemeral and easily transformable digital overlay onto the physical world.

TENSTA KONSTHALL

INTERIOR THAT REVEALS VISITOR BEHAVIOR
AND THE PASSAGE OF TIME
2003

Most built environments undergo a gradual transformation in the natural progression of their life cycle. Some changes are anticipated, while others may be entirely unexpected. Ultimately, people's perceptions and expectations are critical in whether the aging of interior spaces is accepted or rejected. Considered early in the planning of a project, this concept can lead to thoughtful results that rely on external factors such as time and occupation to complete the designer's intent. In a former unused storage space turned contemporary arts center, the designers embraced the reality of surface wear and tear, and of furniture being moved, replaced, or even stolen over time. They took this as an opportunity to create a series of spaces for the center's entrance and café where change was a built-in feature. Not only did they deliberately leverage the inherent temporal nature of interiors through the use of living finishes that evolve with every use, but they also challenged preconceived ideas about interior decoration by combining ubiquitous household items with high design.

Cheap plastic lawn chairs were altered with casters and specially-made leather seats, while fast-growing plants were expected to convert the space into an indoor garden.

The freshly painted floor as it was before being transformed by visitors. On the walls is a custom three-dimensional wallpaper made from silk flowers.

The gray top coat of the two-layer floor finish was intended to wear and reveal the underlying golden color, registering the movements of visitors and leaving behind trace evidence of occupation.

LOCATION: SPÅNGA, SWEDEN
DESIGNER: FRONT (WWW.FRONTDESIGN.SE)
MAJOR PROJECT PARTNERS OR COLLABORATORS: TENSTA KONSTHALL, STOCKHOLMS KOMMUN

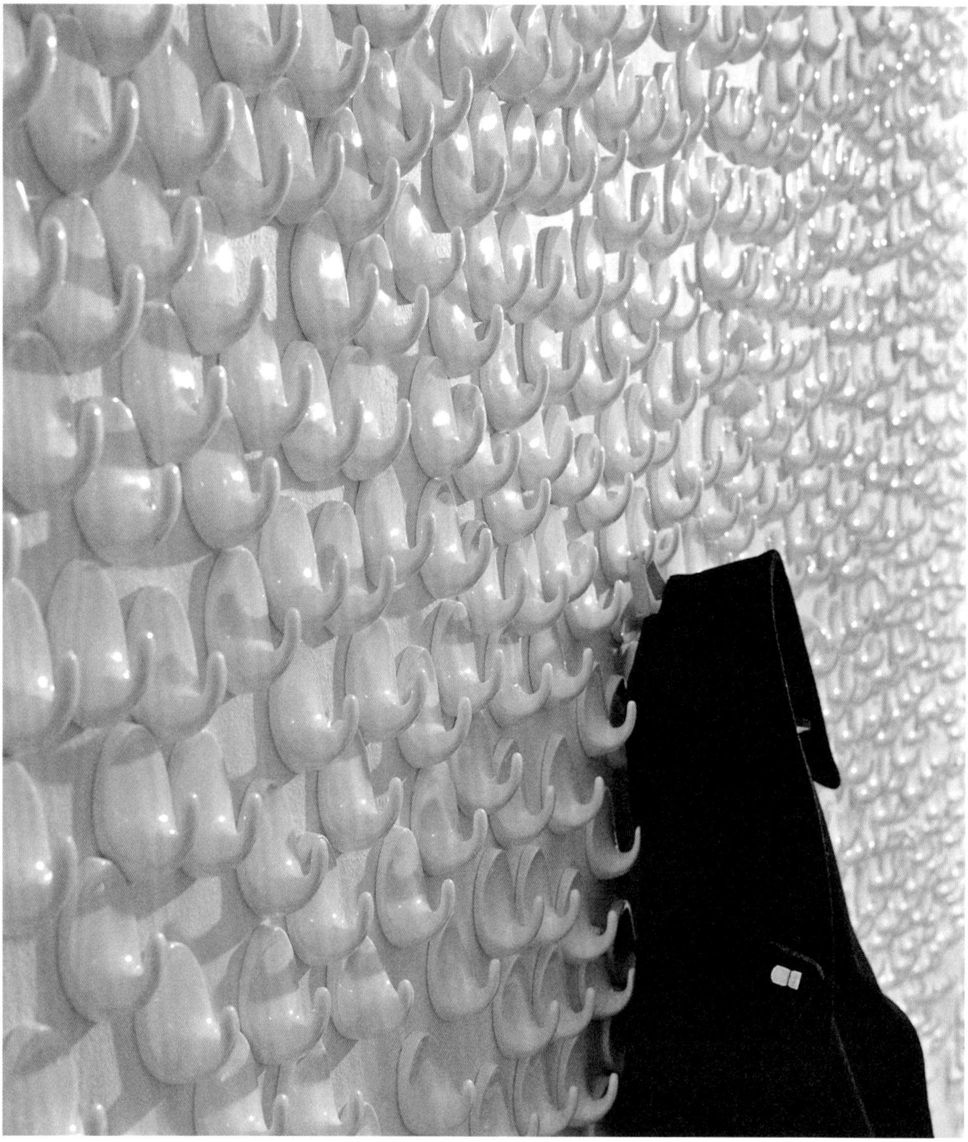

Visitors were invited to add to the expanding collection of self-adhesive plastic hooks in the wardrobe area, with the anticipation that they would eventually cover the entire wall.

A striped pattern painted on the ground extended the gallery space to the outdoors where hundreds of plastic chairs heat-stamped with "Tensta Konsthall" were placed, free to be moved or even taken.

UNDERFULL

TABLECLOTH THAT TURNS EMBARRASSING SPILLS INTO VISUAL POETRY
2009

In many cultures, white tablecloths signal a formal occasion and elicit a particular behavioral response from diners, prompting them to follow etiquette rules and display proper table manners. This seemingly unremarkable tablecloth bearing a traditional white floral damask pattern does just that, but it also conceals a secret. Sooner or later throughout a meal, someone is likely to spill, but where this clumsiness usually results in embarrassment, the person responsible is left feeling pleasantly surprised. Not only does the tablecloth itself transform, but it also has the power to shift a negative situation into a positive experience. Instead of leaving behind an undesirable stain, red wine and other liquids reveal a hidden butterfly pattern within the woven textile. Each stain contributes to a narrative and the tablecloth's sentimental value as its overall pattern evolves, making stain removal unnecessary. This unique design brings depth and a fresh approach that challenges society's superficial relationship with objects used in daily life. The motif was selected by the designer because it represents the incredible metamorphosis that caterpillars undergo before changing into colorful butterflies.

According to the designer, the feathered edges of the spill pattern are reminiscent of a butterfly's fragility and transience.

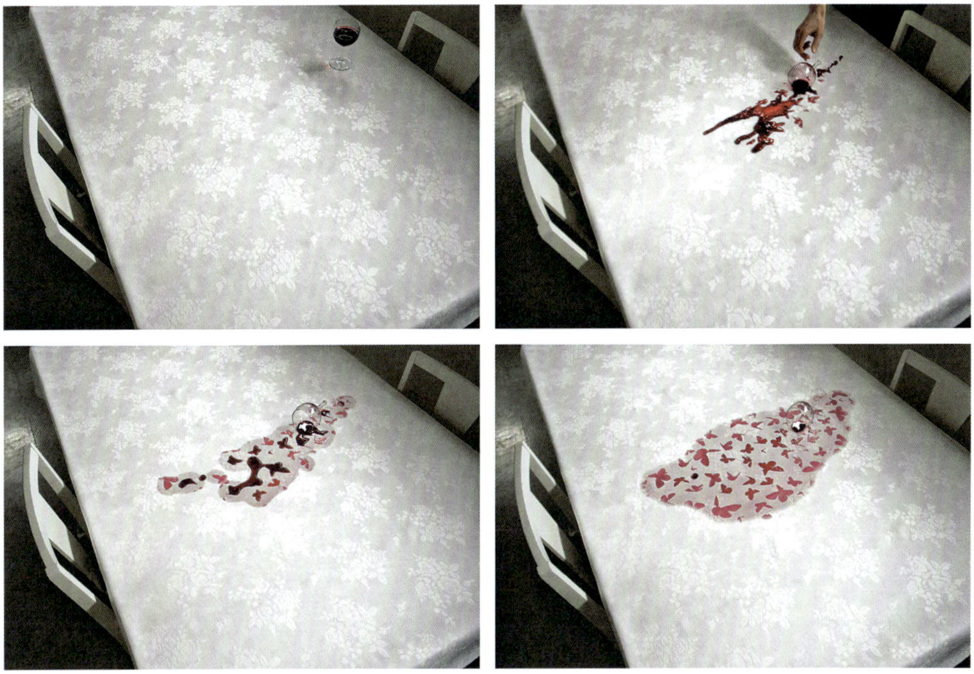

This prototype demonstrates the tablecloth's magical transformation where a colorful pattern is revealed with each spill, allowing its overall aesthetic to evolve.

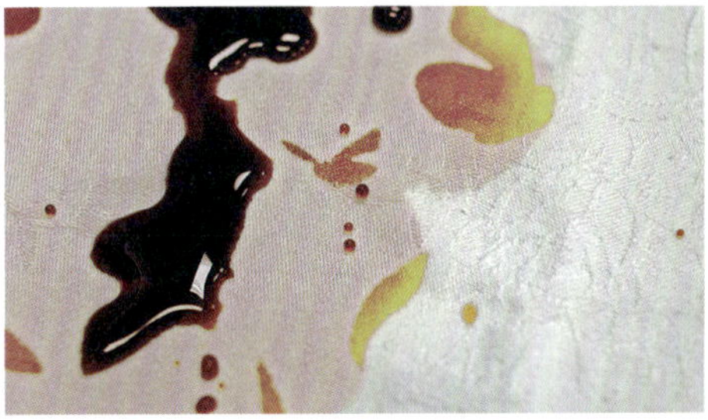

An overlapping pattern of butterflies spreads out over the woven floral pattern, creating a layered effect.

Various liquids leave different colors behind, adding to the visual narrative.

LOCATION: OSLO, NORWAY
DESIGNER: KRISTINE BJAADAL (WWW.KRISTINEBJAADAL.NO)
MAJOR PROJECT PARTNER OR COLLABORATOR: OSLO NATIONAL ACADEMY OF THE ARTS

SOSIA

CONVERTIBLE SOFA THAT ALLOWS THE USER
TO GENERATE A VARIETY OF LIVING SCENARIOS
2011

Modular seating and fold-out sofa beds respond to the need for furniture to be flexible and accommodating for more than one setting or use. Sosia, meaning "double" in Italian, offers an even greater level of versatility. This free-form furniture element allows the user to create different arrangements based on their needs. One may choose to enclose or expose one's activities through the adjustment of a Lycra flap and zipper, which wraps and bends around polyurethane foam cushions. The options vary from a single sofa to two armchairs arranged face-to-face, adjacent, or L-shaped. A semiprivate or fully enclosed daybed is also possible, as is a changing room. Inspired by the designer's own experiences with compact living, Sosia bridges the gap between a piece of furniture and a micro-room. It transforms to precisely fit a behavior or a situation, forming a dynamic relationship between user and furniture that encourages a fluid and responsive approach. Notably, these interactions also leave behind trace evidence, allowing insight into past behaviors and activities that may have taken place in the room based on the furniture's last placement and position.

Orientation and personal distance are important when socializing. Side-by-side and angled seating provide for different types of exchanges depending on how well people know one another and how competitive or noncompetitive the situation.

A contrasting, brightly colored zipper aids in understanding the furniture's adaptable features.

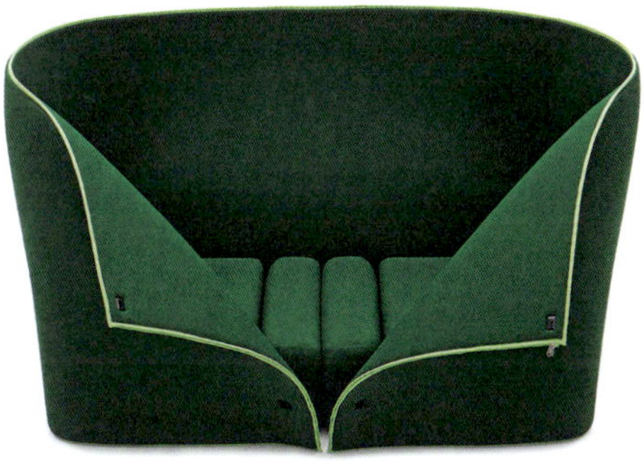

The unit's ability to morph from a piece of furniture to an enclosed space affords varying degrees of privacy for introverted activities such as sleeping and changing clothes to extroverted social gatherings.

LOCATION: MILAN, ITALY
DESIGNER: EMANUELE MAGINI FOR CAMPEGGI (WWW.EMANUELEMAGINI.IT)
MAJOR PROJECT PARTNER OR COLLABORATOR: CAMPEGGI (MANUFACTURING)

SOFTSHELTER

COLLAPSIBLE PARTITIONS THAT PROVIDE TEMPORARY SHELTER AND PRIVACY
2011

Inspired by the need to transform large public venues into relief shelters during times of natural disasters, softshelter is a system for creating adaptable and flexible spaces indoors. The designers developed the concept while planning a cultural center in Japan where one of the requirements was that the building also serve as an emergency shelter. While the design process was underway, Hurricane Katrina forced many people to take refuge in a vast sports stadium, further highlighting the need for such a system. To combat the dehumanizing effects in these circumstances, the designers sought to provide privacy and comfort while also encouraging individuals to begin rebuilding a sense of community. The flexible kraft paper walls can partition a large area into a variety of configurations, quickly providing individuals and families with a zone of personal space. The system's low-tech nature means that it can easily be set up and modified without the need for special tools, enabling occupants to take control over their environment. Additionally, a range of "home-making" and "community" accessories aim to enhance function and offer opportunities for personalization. After its deployment, the system can be flat-packed for efficient shipping or storage.

Softshelter facilitates space-making using soft, flexible materials instead of rigid building blocks.

The walls, which are made from kraft paper treated with a nontoxic fire retardant, employ a flexible honeycomb geometry allowing them to stretch and connect via magnetic end panels.

LOCATION: VANCOUVER, CANADA
DESIGNER: MOLO (WWW.MOLODESIGN.COM)
MAJOR PROJECT PARTNERS OR COLLABORATORS: STEPHANIE FORSYTHE AND TODD MACALLEN (DESIGN)

A participatory process where an employee lived in a softshelter for six weeks led to discoveries for refinement of the system.

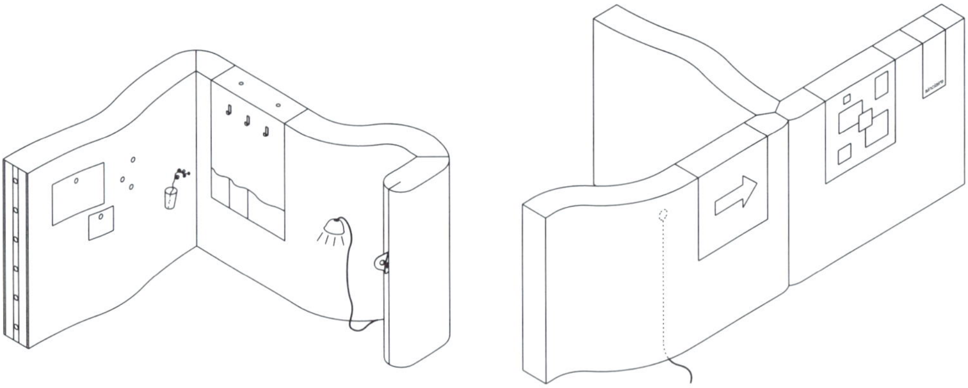

Accessories can aid in wayfinding between units or be used to personalize the shelter's interior, creating a semblance of home.

Insights from inhabiting a mockup informed simple additions like a cardboard tube for hanging clothes and easy-to-grasp felt handles.

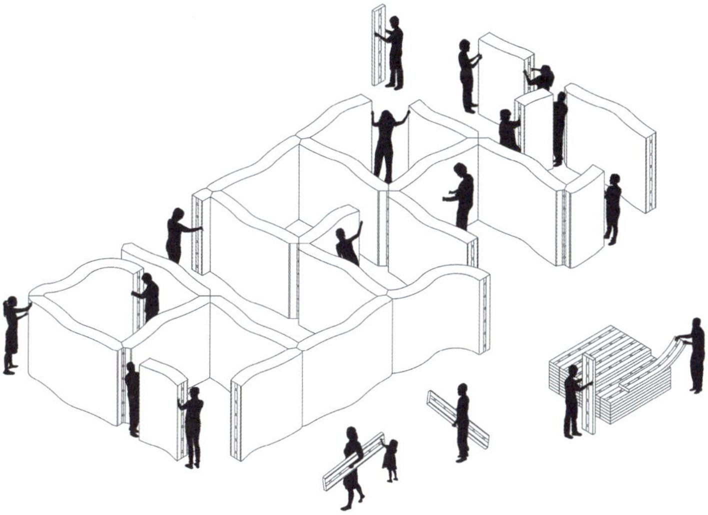

Private living quarters and shared gathering spaces can be created within large arenas and gymnasiums, with the possibility to reshape them as needed.

IMAGINATION PLAYGROUND

TRANSPORTABLE PLAYGROUND THAT ENCOURAGES CHILDREN TO CREATE THEIR OWN PLAY ENVIRONMENTS
2010

Imagination Playground is an open-ended system designed as a series of loose parts that can be combined to create limitless options for play. The initial installation took place in a public park in Lower Manhattan named after the system, Imagination Playground Park. Today, there are over 3,000 installations in the US and abroad. This kit-of-parts approach takes the underlying principles and proven developmental benefits of block play inherent in childhood favorites such as Lincoln Logs and Legos and scales them up to life-size components. Where typical playgrounds contain fixed equipment such as slides, seesaws, and monkey bars that promote prescribed activities, this new concept was conceived to be self-directed and to facilitate play in an unrestricted fashion, fostering creativity, problem-solving, and social interaction. There are no rules, and the playground can be reset and transformed indefinitely. This type of unstructured play, which differs from many toys and games that come with instructions to follow, relies on a child's imagination without dictating how they should play.

The larger scale of the blocks encourages children to play in groups, aiding in the development of cognitive and social skills.

Children create play spaces with loose parts, which is fundamentally different from conventional, fixed playgrounds that focus on developing gross motor skills.

LOCATION: NEW YORK, NY, UNITED STATES (FIRST INSTALLATION, NOW IN OVER 3,000 LOCATIONS)
DESIGNER: THE ROCKWELL GROUP (WWW.ROCKWELLGROUP.COM, WWW.IMAGINATIONPLAYGROUND.COM)
MAJOR PROJECT PARTNERS OR COLLABORATORS: THE ROCKWELL GROUP (DESIGN), KABOOM (PLAY-BASED NOT-FOR-PROFIT), NEW YORK CITY DEPARTMENT OF PARKS AND RECREATION, UNICEF, DISNEY FOUNDATION, LET'S MOVE! BY MICHELLE OBAMA, HUNDREDS OF CHILDREN'S MUSEUMS IN NORTH AMERICA, IMAGINATION PLAYGROUND ADVISORY PANEL

Suitable for both indoor and outdoor applications, the system is flexible and adaptable; however, it is only available in one color to avoid distraction or competition.

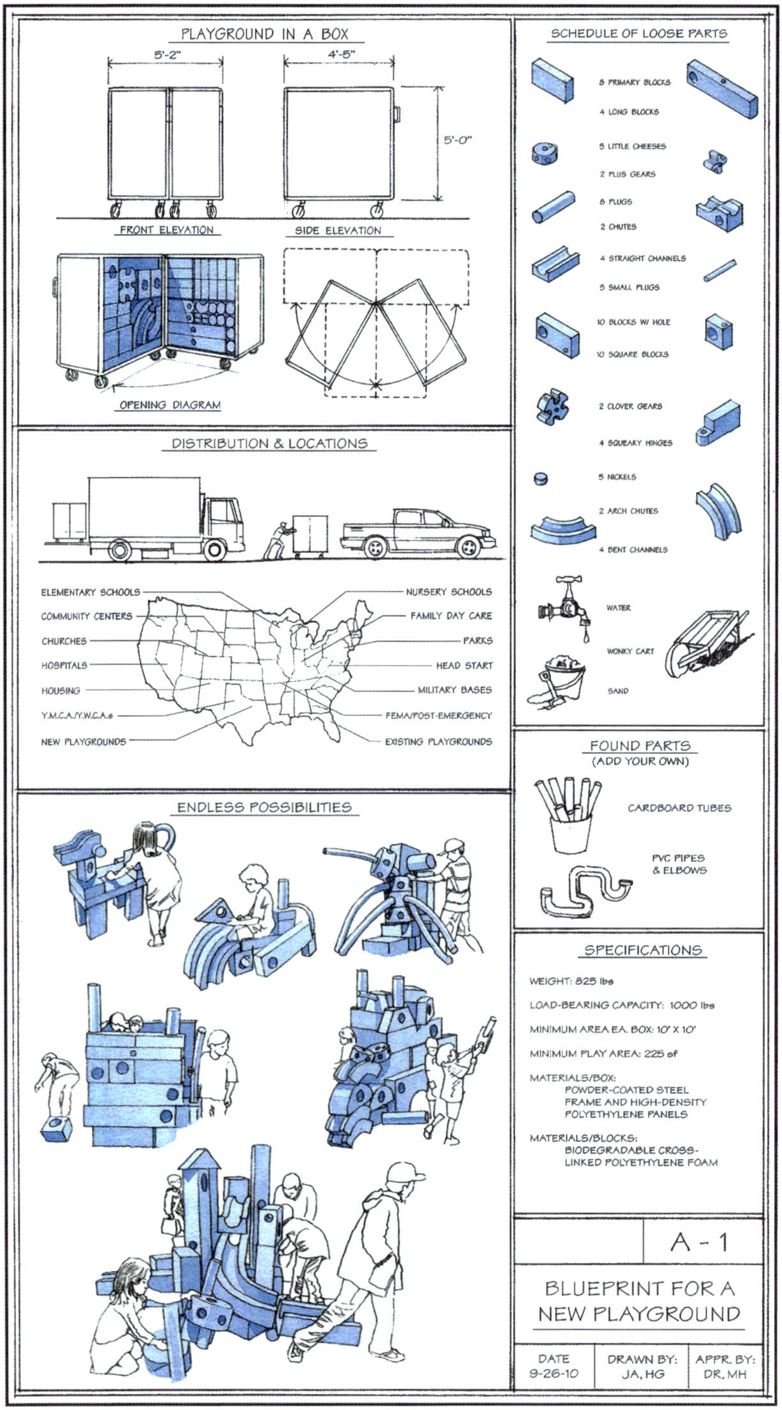

The kit-of-parts comes in many shapes that fit together to form imagined life-size objects and spaces.

Sets are made of antimicrobial, nontoxic foam and are transported and stored in boxes, carts, or "drag bags." At the end of their lifespan, they can be returned to the manufacturer and recycled.

WELCOME HOME

BLANK ROOM THAT TRANSPORTS VISITORS
TO PLACES AROUND THE GLOBE
2015

This branded experience took the form of a temporary installation titled "Welcome Home," created for Airbnb Singapore. With the rise of the sharing economy, Airbnb's business concept has spread internationally, connecting hosts and travelers, but Singaporeans have been skeptical of the idea. They tend to prefer staying in luxury hotels when traveling abroad rather than renting strangers' homes. The designers aimed to convey the benefits of the Airbnb experience that allows tourists to travel and see new places and live like a local. To do this, they used augmented reality, which is a physical environment that is digitally enhanced, blending the real with the virtual. Projection artists, architects, and interior designers collaborated to recreate actual Airbnb property listings from various countries, which were mapped onto a blank interior. The immersive result enabled visitors to experience these accommodations without leaving Singapore. While not a perfect substitute, the speed and ease of transforming an interior through augmented reality is an intriguing concept that generates authentic emotive qualities.

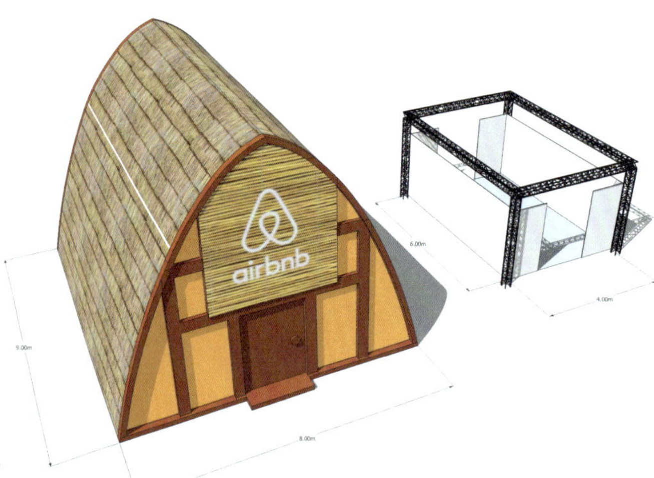

Beneath the exterior cladding, a theater stage truss system supported the room-sized augmented reality installation.

The transportive experience, housed within a temporary pavilion reminiscent of a Balinese hut, was part of Singapore Design Week.

LOCATION: SINGAPORE
DESIGNER: THE GOVT (WWW.THEGOVT.ORG)
MAJOR PROJECT PARTNERS OR COLLABORATORS: THE GOVT (CREATIVE AGENCY), UNTITLED PROJECT (PROJECTION MAPPING/ANIMATED CONTENT)

Four Airbnb listings from Bali, Penang, Paris, and Tokyo were projection-mapped onto the interior walls and furnishings, conveying the unique identity of each place.

A host answered visitors' questions within the blank room containing all-white furniture, which then became the backdrop for the projection of architectural features, finishes, and décor.

Designers paid close attention to details such as virtual windows with animated views and interior accents including a working wall clock and an oscillating fan.

CHAPTER **6**

CHALLENGING PROVOCATION

DEFINITION: The act of an object or environment that incites feelings, desires, or activities with the intent to test social and cultural norms

People have learned over time what is considered appropriate and culturally accepted conduct within certain environments, and there are corresponding conventions as to how one "should" act in a library, church, or theater. Described as the behavior-setting theory, public places or even occasions can induce certain patterns of behavior. These instances become small-scale social systems, and the surrounding spaces are typically arranged to suit. The examples in this category challenge traditional norms and behavior settings and attempt to either create a new normal or to force the user to see the environment afresh from their worldview. A designer's success in accomplishing this requires an acute understanding of conventions to reconsider, test, and subsequently challenge them. Social learning theory explains how occupants of these unique environments must then observe others in the altered scenario and adjust their actions accordingly. Several strategies can be employed to develop a project into a challenging provocation. The fundamentals of one type of built environment can be transferred to a different environment, expected elements or design features of a space can be exchanged for the less predictable, or known social constructs can be tested.

STRATEGY: TYPOLOGY TRANSFER

Typologies of buildings, spaces, and even furniture often lend themselves to anticipated behaviors, which result in a standard set of physical design features. Furthermore, designers and firms may become known for their expertise in a particular typology or market sector, and they indeed do bring substantial knowledge to these projects. At times though, it can be helpful to see spaces anew when seeking to create an innovative environment. Typologies can become staid to the point that few people question them, regardless of whether or not there are opportunities for improvement. Thankfully, the boundaries between typologies have become increasingly blurred in recent years, and this is resulting in inspired spaces. Healthcare design, for example, has borrowed successfully from hospitality and restaurant design by paying more attention to the overall experience to such an extent that it is becoming the new standard. The further the stretch from one type to another, the more challenging the impact. In the same way that one may nimbly think of technology transfer, consider the idea of typology transfer.

In the case study of a historic church building that houses a bookstore (Selexyz Dominicanen, p. 192), there are several factors at work. The behavior setting of a church and that of a bookstore, which can be similar to a library, tend to both be quiet and contemplative. They also have similar physical features in that repetitive rows and tables of books with clear circulation paths are not all that different from pews separated by aisles. So, why is this such a challenging leap? Deep-rooted views hold churches as sacred and commerce as the antithesis. Enjoying a coffee in the café located in the choir near the former altar gives the impression of being a sacrilege, which sets the scene for spatial and behavioral tension.

On the other hand, cross-referencing other disciplines can be motivational when creating a challenging environment. People have expectations about what constitutes inside and outside, and the threshold between seems to be an enduring fascination, while many believe that there are health and well-being benefits to biophilic design. What does an outdoor room look and feel like, and how might a large open interior be more like a landscape? Here, the example of a workplace that has more in common with a greenhouse than an office (Offices of Pons + Huot, p. 198), treats the design of the interior like exterior site design. The ground floor plane is raised to create subterranean spaces, and trees emerge from the same surfaces as desk lamps.

STRATEGY: ELEMENT EXCHANGE

Typology transfer implies a large move, but sometimes determining what is most characteristic of a particular type of space and identifying one element or feature to challenge can also be effective. It may mean following the convention for all other aspects so that the atypical quality truly stands out. In the beginning, it can be useful to ask big picture questions. What type of behavior should and could this space support? How is this typically accomplished? What elements, in particular, are involved? Then, consider what might happen if one of these elements took another form, was replaced by something else, or functioned differently. In retrospect, the most successful disruptions are easy to identify, but it is important to keep an open mind and ask these seemingly basic questions on the front end of the design process.

In the case of museums, familiar ways of organizing galleries and viewing art yield predictable behavior patterns. However, what if the aim is to interrupt this rhythm and encourage visitors to dwell longer and in a more relaxed state? In one such example (Textile Field, p. 202), this was accomplished by removing the conventional benches and replacing them with a bed-like raised platform. This exchange did not physically alter the museum or the display of art, but it did completely transform visitors' responses. The platform was less prescriptive than recognizable furnishings that have defined uses. Visitors had to observe how others were reacting to it rather than rely on customary social cues to navigate the gallery.

Understanding assumptions and expectations are vital to the process. For example, one presumes that settings like homes and hotels will offer a gradient of public and private space. It is a given that these typologies will address this issue, and occupants will be able to modulate their level of privacy through various features. In one city overrun by tourism, a pop-up accommodation (Temporary Hotel, p. 206) put this matter on display by removing the guests' "right" to privacy in their rooms, calling attention to a societal problem facing the community. Something as simple as omitting window treatments exposed guests in a way that dramatically changed their actions and ultimately their level of comfort.

STRATEGY: SOCIAL CONSTRUCT TEST

A social construct is a phenomenon created by the influence of society. It could be a belief or a perception held by individuals or a group of people and entrenched within a culture. Regardless of whether or not it reflects reality, it may dictate which behaviors or practices are considered acceptable or taboo. Pinpointing the crux of a social construct and assessing how it relates to the surrounding context can provide clues on how the built environment can disrupt and challenge this point of view.

What might be regarded as reasonable or appropriate in one setting may not be in another. For example, intimacy is not usually a concern in the design of workplaces. However, nearly every corporate culture has some inherent competitiveness and hierarchy. How could the design of office furniture challenge this notion and support closeness and cooperation instead? One example (The Love Seat, p. 212) encourages co-workers to sit side-by-side and make eye contact in the way that courting couples did centuries ago. Imagine how this orientation and proximity could impact a performance review between a supervisor and their subordinate compared to the same meeting around a formal conference table.

In another instance, a person sitting alone reading a book at a coffee shop does not seem out of the ordinary, but the same person seated on their own at a fine dining establishment is perceived quite differently. One restaurant (EENMAAL, p. 214) rejects this social construct by only offering tables for single diners. Here, the goal is to expose, challenge, and transform the idea that this is somehow publicly undesirable.

Not all built environments are necessarily suited to be challenging. For example, it may be apt for an exhibition to be provocative, but likely not for a hospital emergency room. That said, adding these strategies to any design process could prove helpful. The questions one must ask about what an environment should and could be are valuable, even if the result is not intended to make people stop and take notice. These strategies may simply be used to test whether a design has been fully considered and is benefiting from capturing insights from even the most unlikely places. They will also lead to a better understanding of a project's social context and how it may be aided or obstructed by deeply ingrained views and beliefs.

SELEXYZ DOMINICANEN

FORMER CHURCH
THAT HOUSES A BOOKSTORE
2007

There are learned behaviors that coincide with public places such as churches, so it is understandable that visitors may be disoriented when entering a Gothic church converted into a bookstore. Although this is not the first time the building is being used for purposes other than worship. In fact, it has not hosted a religious function since 1794 when Napoleon's army confiscated it. Over the years, it has served as a municipal archive, a warehouse, and even bike storage. Now as a retail outlet, it is far from its original intent at its consecration in 1294 by the Order of Predicators founded by St. Dominic. Given the long-held Christian view that consumerism is amoral, the bookstore and café seem incongruent with the structure. Additionally, the newly inserted interior features—especially the grand bookcase—are purposefully juxtaposed against the centuries-old backdrop. Other design aspects such as the café furnishings are irreverent in form and placement and conjure up unexpected religious associations. This unorthodox and dramatic space has become a destination welcoming around 700,000 visitors a year.

LOCATION: MAASTRICHT, NETHERLANDS
DESIGNER: MERK X, FORMERLY MERKX+GIROD (WWW.MERK-X.NL)
MAJOR PROJECT PARTNERS OR COLLABORATORS: EVELYNE MERKX, PATRICE GIROD, BERT DE MUNNIK, ABBIE STEINHAUSER, JOSJE KUIPER, PIM HOUBEN, RAMON WIJSMAN, AND RUBEN BUS OF MERKX+GIROD (ARCHITECTURE); SATIJNPLUS ARCHITECTEN (RESTAURANT ARCHITECTURE); HANS WOLFF + PARTNERS AND ANSORG (LIGHTING)
THE BUILDING IS NOW UNDER NEW OWNERSHIP

The multilevel bookcase takes full advantage of the church's height with elevated platforms that reveal new vantage points to experience the grand vaults and historic murals.

The monumental scale of the bookcase, which houses a series of integral staircases, matches the church's grand proportions.

The raised seating area for the in-store café follows the curved line of the choir and is anchored by a crucifix-shaped table.

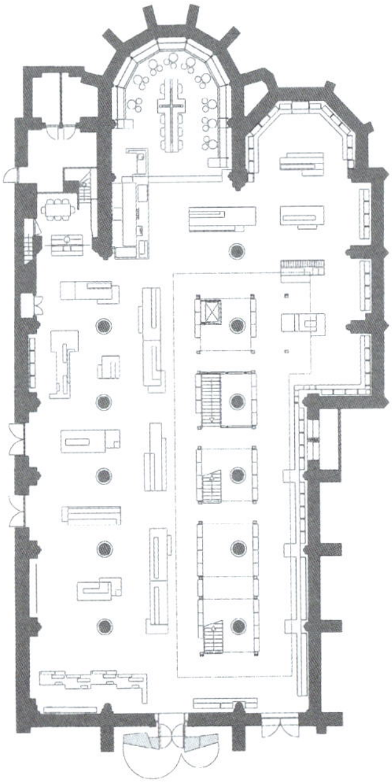

With only 750 m² (8,073 ft²) in the existing church, the inserted bookcase creates additional floor area to fulfill the original brief requiring 1,200 m² (12,917 ft²) of retail.

The asymmetrically-placed modern steel construction encompasses one row of stone columns and provides contrast to the surrounding traditional materials.

The church was home to a flower show around the turn of the 19th century, which is just one of the many secular uses of this building.

OFFICES OF PONS + HUOT

OPEN OFFICE THAT CREATES
AN UNCONVENTIONAL INTERIOR LANDSCAPE
2006

Two companies share a space in this highly unusual setting realized within a late 19th-century industrial hall that was in need of renovation. Rather than subdividing the large open space with typical floors and walls, the designers employed a more novel approach. The primary organization is oriented around a central wooden mass, which is constructed as a thickened ground plane within the interior. Instead of more common furniture solutions, built-in workstations are seemingly carved out of the oak unit, while communal spaces such as meeting areas, a recreational room, kitchen, and restrooms are embedded within it. Large trees dispersed among the central open work area create the feeling of an interior landscape. Appearing as bubbles on the horizon, another unexpected design feature is the incorporation of futuristic-looking acrylic domes at individual workstations to give employees privacy for phone conversations. The otherworldly impression of this space defies convention—a surprise to be discovered within an unsuspecting, traditional steel structure.

There is no reception desk to greet visitors. Instead, other environmental cues guide them along a perimeter walkway leading to key guest spaces.

Individual private offices with full height glass walls face one another, overlooking the raised open work area in the atrium.

LOCATION: PARIS, FRANCE
DESIGNER: CHRISTIAN POTTGIESSER ARCHITECTURESPOSSIBLES / CPAP (WWW.POTTGIESSER.FR)
MAJOR PROJECT PARTNERS OR COLLABORATORS: CHRISTIAN POTTGIESSER AND PASCALE POTTGIESSER (ARCHITECTURE AND VISUAL ARTS)

Behavioral residue, such as office utensils and papers, is a testament to human occupation in the open work area.

Skylights provide daylight and a visual connection in a subterranean conference room.

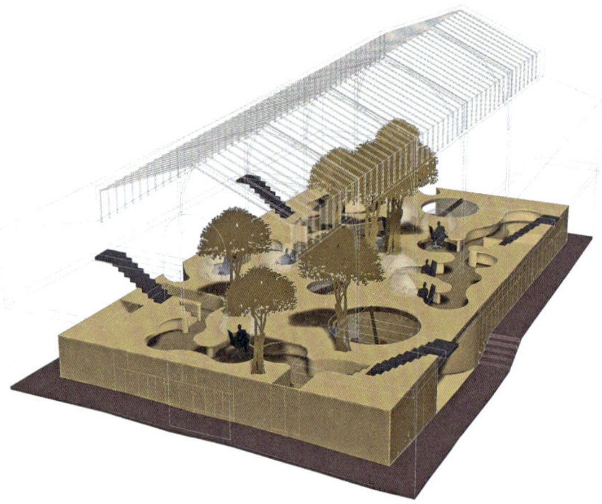

The design is conceptually an oversized piece of furniture inserted into the space, measuring 1.7 m (6.5 ft) high, 22 m (72 ft) long, and 14 m (46 ft) wide.

Built-in workstations are located among tall ficus trees. Some include acrylic domes for acoustic control.

TEXTILE FIELD

RAISED PLATFORM THAT ENCOURAGES VISITORS
TO VIEW ARTWORK FROM A DIFFERENT PERSPECTIVE
2011

Cultural norms determine acceptable behavior in public, thus setting etiquette codes for places such as museums, libraries, and churches. In museums, it is customary to see people walking alone or in small groups, quietly passing through galleries in a state of mind that ranges from contemplation to boredom, with only occasional opportunities for respite. A brief intervention at the Victoria & Albert Museum during the London Design Festival called this worldview into question. For a few days, visitors had the opportunity to appreciate paintings by Italian Renaissance artist Raphael while in postures more akin to sitting and relaxing in an outdoor park. Situated amidst these national treasures was a soft, bed-like structure that interrupted the space and invited viewers to not only stand and sit, but to lie down for a more sensual and dreamlike experience. Abandoning conventional furniture typologies

Measuring 30 m (98 ft) long by 8 m (26 ft) wide, the temporary installation covered a large area of the gallery's existing 600 m^2 (6,458 ft^2) mosaic floor.

From a distance, upholstery in graduating shades of blue and green fabric form a contemporary interpretation of a Renaissance landscape.

with uses that are culturally predefined, the designers introduced a viewing platform that inspired a broader interpretation. The installation lent a casual atmosphere to an otherwise formal space and liberated visitors to temporarily engage in behaviors that disregarded the institutionalized body-in-space relationship expected between art and observer.

More comfortable postures encouraged visitors to stay longer, allowing the gallery to become a backdrop.

The V&A's Raphael Gallery typically offers traditional furniture where people sit back-to-back on centrally placed wooden benches.

The expansive tactile surface evoked a more relaxed and playful mood than usually experienced in museum galleries.

LOCATION: LONDON, UNITED KINGDOM
DESIGNERS: RONAN & ERWAN BOUROULLEC FOR KVADRAT (WWW.BOUROULLEC.COM)
MAJOR PROJECT PARTNER OR COLLABORATOR: KVADRAT (MANUFACTURING)

TEMPORARY HOTEL (NIGHT AT THE MUSEUMLAAN)

TRANSPARENT HOTEL THAT CHALLENGES PRIVACY
FOR GUESTS AND PASSERSBY
2010

The Enschede neighborhood of Roombeek made international headlines for a calamity that occurred in 2000 when a fireworks warehouse exploded. This event subsequently led to disaster tourism within the region, followed by architectural tourism as rebuilding of the neighborhood began. Locals often felt that they were on display and viewed the influx of visitors as a nuisance. In response, an architect and artist team collaborated on a pavilion for the GrensWerk Festival of the Arts, which took the form of a hotel. Unlike most art installations, the temporary hotel building was continuously on view and occupied by guests during the three-week period of the festival. It was constructed entirely of birch plywood and featured large windows with fixed vertical wood slats surrounding the perimeter. The minimal interiors of the bedrooms were stripped of any controls for privacy typically available in a hotel, such as curtains or shades, and were only shielded by a fixed exterior screen. Depending on the time of day, viewing angle, and lighting conditions, hotel guests and passersby took turns being observers. The restrictive and theatrical nature of the project called attention to a particular set of behaviors, intentionally creating awkwardness to initiate dialogue about an uncomfortable situation.

LOCATION: ENSCHEDE, NETHERLANDS
DESIGNER: IAA ARCHITECTS (WWW.IAA-ARCHITECTEN.COM)
MAJOR PROJECT PARTNERS OR COLLABORATORS:
MARKO MATIC AND RICK BRUGGINK OF IAA (ARCHITECTURE), JAN SMAGA AND ANETA GRZESZYKOWSKA (VISUAL ARTS)

The temporary hotel occupied a vacant lot between modern houses designed by well-known architects.

Employing fixed wood slats, the installation questioned notions of privacy.

The simple wood structure was designed to allow for a full view of the guest rooms after dark from the nearby sidewalk and street.

The bedrooms were void of any form of interior window covering, limiting the occupants' control over their privacy.

During the daytime, the structure appeared more opaque.

In the mornings, guests came together for breakfast and the opportunity to share their unusual overnight experiences

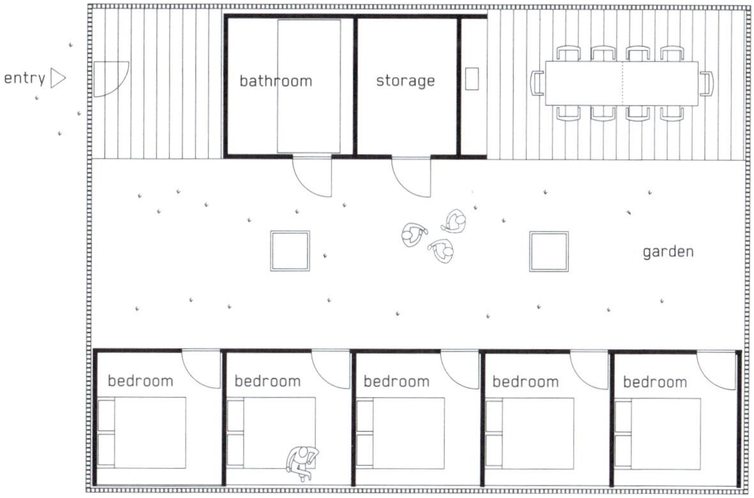

A single architectural volume housed five bedrooms, a shared garden, and guest facilities.

THE LOVE SEAT

SEATING THAT SUPPORTS
INTIMATE WORKPLACE MEETINGS
2015

At first glance, the Love Seat appears to be two chairs pulled up alongside one another. On closer inspection, though, it is revealed to be one piece of furniture with conjoined seating surfaces and a mutual armrest. Its detailing and shared structure subtly imply a sense of personal connection. The form takes its cue from a particular variety of love seat known as a tête-à-tête, which historically supported face-to-face conversation between courting individuals without physical contact. However, this contemporary version was designed especially for a workplace environment. The co-workers' orientation and physical proximity to one another while sitting in the Love Seat imply partnership, thus contesting the competitive nature of many corporate cultures.

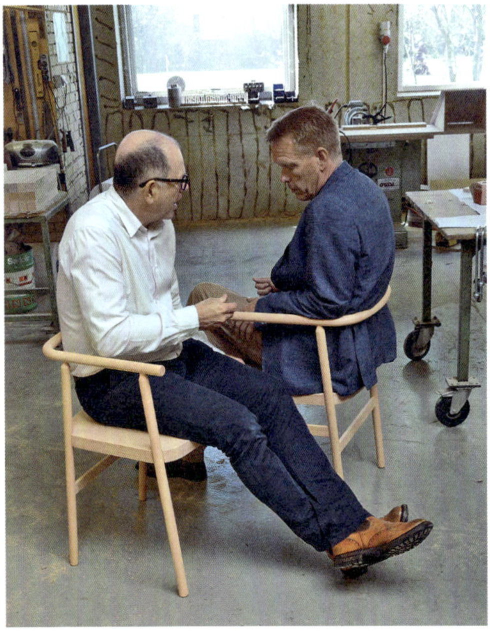

The Love Seat's design intent is only achieved when two people sit in it together.

Sketches offer insight into the designers' exploration of the side-by-side orientation with various armrest and seat details.

Crafted using traditional materials and techniques, the Love Seat embodies both the expected and unexpected.

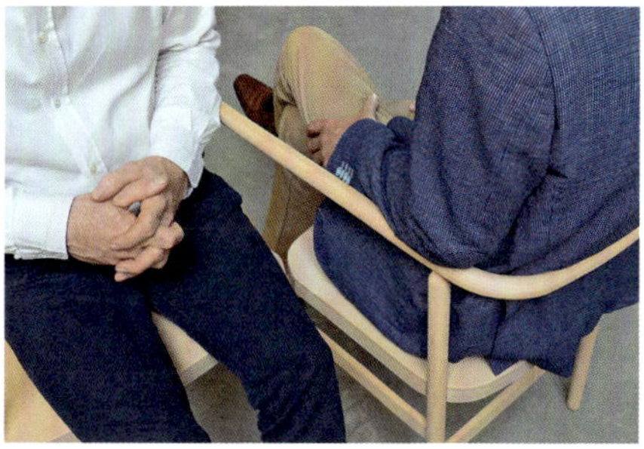

The shared armrest allows both occupants to support their elbows without interference while also defining boundaries.

This level of intimacy is not typical of the often-sterile environment of contemporary workplaces. The Love Seat provides equality for two people to make eye contact and ultimately establish a rapport while natural materials offer a contrast to today's high-tech environments filled with synthetic finishes. The self-proclaimed "smallest meeting space you could invent" also tests the westernized view of personal distances by placing a work colleague within one's intimate distance zone, described by the anthropologist Edward T. Hall in *The Hidden Dimension* as ranging from direct contact to 46 cm (18 in). The designers not only aimed to challenge traditional furniture typologies but also conventional ideas about workplace design and interaction to create a healthier and more humane approach to work.

LOCATION: LONDON, UNITED KINGDOM
DESIGNER: PEARSONLLOYD FOR TEKNION (WWW.PEARSONLLOYD.COM)
MAJOR PROJECT PARTNER OR COLLABORATOR: TEKNION (MANUFACTURING)

EENMAAL

RESTAURANT THAT ONLY HAS TABLES
TO SEAT SINGLE DINERS
2013

Many people share the common belief that dining alone in public is associated with loneliness and thus attempt to avoid it. Restaurant designs typically further reinforce the idea of togetherness by offering tables for two, four, or more. Solo diners sitting among empty chairs feel the presence of absence, which calls attention to the ingrained cultural attitude that dining out is mostly driven by the desire for social interaction. Rarely, if ever, are options provided for single diners, who often end up at communal tables or bar seating, which by design implies a level of social engagement with strangers. EENMAAL, which means both "one time" and "one meal," is a pop-up restaurant that seeks to destigmatize solitary dining by only offering tables for one. The concept's designer cites the philosopher Jean-Paul Sartre, who stated, "If you are lonely when you are alone, you are in bad company."[1] In this temporary social experiment, guests have permission to be on their own and momentarily disconnect from a hyperconnected world. With Wi-Fi access blocked, diners are encouraged to savor the culinary experience while reading physical books and magazines, writing, sketching, or listening to music without the constant distractions of others—either in person or virtually; a concept that is becoming increasingly more relevant.

1 Jean-Paul Sartre, *Essays in Aesthetics* (New York: Philosophical Library, 2012) 16.

Shopfront windows of the former supermarket put diners on display with the aim of eliminating the social stigma of dining alone.

The seating arrangement prevents diners from sitting directly across from one another.

LOCATION: AMSTERDAM, NETHERLANDS (FIRST INSTALLATION)
DESIGNER: MARINA VAN GOOR CREATIVE AGENCY MVGCA (WWW.MVGCA.NL)
MAJOR PROJECT PARTNERS OR COLLABORATORS: MARINA VAN GOOR (SOCIAL DESIGN), VANDEJONG (GRAPHIC IDENTITY)

The lack of dinner table conversations encourages diners to focus on the four-course meal.

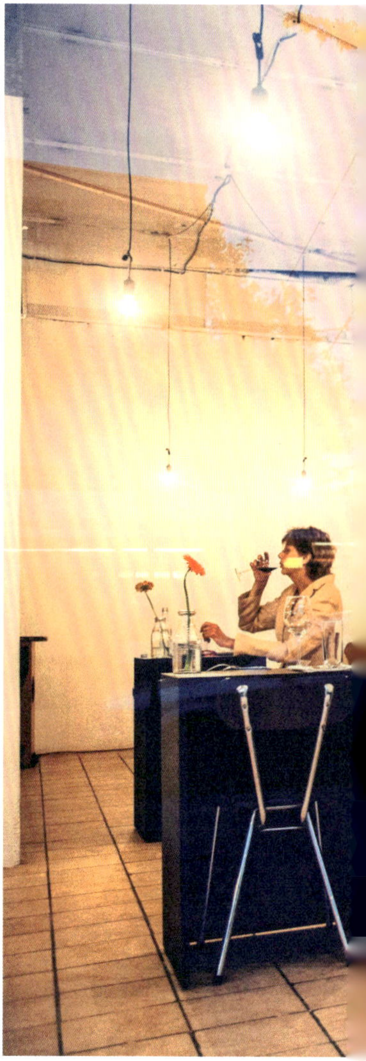

The exclusive use of single tables reinforces the concept of solitary dining, forging a more positive image of solo dining practices.

BIBLIOGRAPHY

INTRODUCTION

"Antenna™ Workspaces." Antenna Design New York, Inc. 2010. Web. March 2018.

"Can Robots Have Social Intelligence?" *Microsoft Research Blog.* Microsoft 2014. Web. May 2017.

"Inclusive Design: Definitions." Design and Architecture Norway. 2010. Web. March 2018.

"Look and Feel." Technopedia Inc. 2018. Web. March 2018.

"Number of Monthly Active Pinterest Users from September 2015 to September 2017." Statista, Inc. 2018. Web. March 2018.

Bobrow, Emily. "The Innovation Insurrection." *Perspective* 2015: 12–19. Print.

Budds, Diana. "9 Ideas Shaping the Future of Design, According to Ideo, Microsoft, Autodesk, MIT, and More." Co.Design by Mansueto Ventures. 2017. Web. March 2018.

Dilger, Daniel Eran. "Iphone Patent Wars: Xerox Parc & the Apple, Inc. Macintosh: Innovator, Duplicator & Litigator." Quiller Media, Inc. 2013. Web. March 2018.

Fox, Michael. *Interactive Architecture: Adaptive World.* New York: Princeton Architectural Press, 2016. Print.

Fox, Michael, and Miles Kemp. *Interactive Architecture.* New York: Princeton Architectural Press, 2009. Print.

Gensler Research Institute. *Gensler Experience Index.* Gensler, 2017. Print.

Hassenzahl, Marc. *Experience Design: Technology for All the Right Reasons.* Synthesis Lectures on Human-Centered Informatics. Ed. Carroll, John M. Morgan & Claypool Publishers, 2010. Print.

Hassenzahl, Marc, et al. "Designing Moments of Meaning and Pleasure. Experience Design and Happiness." *International Journal of Design* 7.3 (2013): 21–31. Print.

Heath, Chip, and Dan Heath. "Thinking in Moments." *The Power of Moments: Why Certain Experiences Have Extraordinary Impact.* New York: Simon & Schuster, 2017. Print.

Ishii, Hiroshi, and Brygg Ullmer. "Tangible Bits: Towards Seamless Interfaces between People, Bits and Atoms." *CHI '97.* Proc. of ACM SIGCHI Conference on Human Factors in Computing Systems, Atlanta. New York: ACM, 1997. 234–41. Print.

Kinchin, Juliet, and Aidan O'Connor. *Counter Space: Design and the Modern Kitchen.* New York: The Museum of Modern Art, 2011. Print.

Kopec, Dak. *Environmental Psychology for Design.* New York: Fairchild Publications, Inc., 2006. Print.

Lupton, Ellen. "Designing for People." *Beautiful Users: Designing for People.* New York: Princeton Architectural Press and Cooper Hewitt Smithsonian Design Museum, 2014. Print.

Martin, Bella, and Bruce Hanington. *Universal Methods of Design: 100 Ways to Research Complex Problems, Develop Innovative Ideas and Design Effective Solutions.* Beverly, Massachusetts: Rockport Publishers, 2012. Print.

Martin, Olivia. "How Are Image-Sharing Apps Affecting Architecture and Design?" *The Architect's Newspaper.* 2018. Web. March 2018.

Morrow-Howell, Nancy, and Sarah Gehlert. "Social Engagement and a Healthy Aging Society." *Public Health for an Aging Society.* Eds. Prohaska, Thomas R., Lynda A. Anderson and Robert H. Binstock. Baltimore, Maryland: The Johns Hopkins University Press, 2012. 205–26. Print.

Norman, Don. *The Design of Everyday Things.* New York: Basic Books, 2013. Print.

Patten, James. "Architecting Experience." Patten Studio. 2018. Web. March 2018.

Patten, James. "The Convergence of Interaction Design and Architecture." *DesignIntelligence Quarterly.* 23. Third Quarter (2017): 28–30. Web. March 2018.

Pine, B. Joseph II, and James Gilmore. "Welcome to the Experience Economy." *Harvard Business Review* 76.4 (1998): 97–106. Print.

Rittel, Horst W. J., and Melvin M. Webber. "Dilemmas in a General Theory of Planning." *Policy Sciences* 4.2 (1973): 155–69. Print.

Rolston, Mark. "The Future of Smart Things Is Dumb." Co.Design by Mansueto Ventures. 2014. Web. March 2018.

Simon, Nina. "Social Objects." *The Participatory Museum.* Santa Cruz, California: Museum 2.0, 2010. Print.

Steenson, Molly Wright. *Architectural Intelligence: How Designers and Architects Created the Digital Landscape.* MIT Press, 2017. Print.

Steenson, Molly Wright, and Fred Scharmen. "Architecture Needs to Interact: If Architectural Practice Kept Pace with Interaction Design, What New Visions of the World Might Appear?" *Domus* December (2011). Web. December 2017.

Stinson, Elizabeth. "Cramped Apartment? Try Some Transforming, Robotic Furniture." WIRED by Condé Nast. 2017. Web. March 2018.

Stokols, Daniel. "The Paradox of Environmental Psychology." *American Psychologist* 50.10 (1995): 821–37. Print.

Wigglesworth, Sarah, and Jeremy Till. "The Everyday and Architecture." *Architectural Design* 1998: 6–9. Print.

Wilson, Mark. "Want to Design Great Digital Experiences? Start Working with Architects." Co.Design by Mansueto Ventures. 2018. Web. January 2018.

CHAPTER 1: INTUITIVE COMMUNICATION

"Affordance." *Merriam-Webster.* Merriam-Webster Inc. 2017. Web. December 2017.

"Infocomm Investments—Singapore Offices." Office Snapshots, LLC. Web. April 2018.

Antonelli, Paola. *Talk to Me: Design and the Communication between People and Objects.* New York: The Museum of Modern Art, 2011. Print.

Disalvo, Carl, and Francine Gemperle. "From Seduction to Fulfillment: The Use of Anthropomorphic Form in Design." *DPPI '03.* Proc. of International Conference on Designing Pleasurable Products and Interfaces, Pittsburgh. New York: ACM, 2003. 67–72. Print.

Emmons, Paul. "The Cosmogony of Bubble Diagrams." *Constructing Identity: Souped-up and Un-plugged.* Proc. of 86th ACSA Annual Meeting and Technology Conference. Washington, DC: Association of Collegiate Schools of Architecture, 1998. 420–25. Print.

Frearson, Amy. "Training Dresser by Peter Bristol." Dezeen Ltd. 2011. Web. March 2018.

Future-Shape. *Sensfloor® System Catalog—January 2017.* Höhenkirchen-Siegertsbrunn: Future-Shape GmbH, 2017. 1–20. Print.

Golovanov, Sly. "Ikea Concept Kitchen 2025." YouTube LLC. 2015. Web. March 2018.

Hallnäs, Lars, and Johan Redström. "From Use to Presence: On the Expressions and Aesthetics of Everyday

Computational Things." *ACM Transactions on Computer-Human Interaction* 9.2 (2002): 106–24. Print.
Hallnäs, Lars, and Johan Redström. *Interaction Design: Foundations, Experiments.* Sweden: The Interactive Institute, The Swedish School of Textiles, University College of Borås, 2006. Print.
Hussey, Matt. "Sensfloor Conductive Rug by Future-Shape Turns the Floor into a Giant Touchscreen." Dezeen Ltd. 2014. Web. July 2017.
Ishii, Hiroshi, and Brygg Ullmer. "Tangible Bits: Towards Seamless Interfaces between People, Bits and Atoms." *CHI '97.* Proc. of ACM SIGCHI Conference on Human Factors in Computing Systems, Atlanta. New York: ACM, 1997. 234–41. Print.
Jafarinaimi, Nassim, et al. "Breakaway: An Ambient Display Designed to Change Human Behavior." *CHI '05 Extended Abstracts on Human Factors in Computing Systems.* Proc. of CHI 2005 Conference on Human Factors in Computing Systems, Portland, OR. New York: ACM, 2005. 1945–48. Print.
Keller, Michael. "Advanced Flooring Turns Whole Rooms into Touchscreens for Monitoring Movement." Txchnologist by General Electric 2014. Web. July 2017.
Kulper, Amy Catania. "Encountering the List: Georges Perec and the Archive as Spatial Paradigm." *Candide—Journal for Architectural Knowledge* 3.12 (2010): 137–67. Print.
Lamy, Lubomir, Jacques Fischer-Lokou, and Nicolas Guéguen. "Valentine Street Promotes Chivalrous Helping." *Swiss Journal of Psychology* 69.3 (2010): 169–72. Print.
Lockton, Dan, et al. "Influencing Interaction: Development of the Design with Intent Method." *Persuasive '09.* Proc. of 4th International Conference on Persuasive Technology, Claremont, California. New York: ACM, 2009. Article No. 5. Print.
Lynch, Kevin. *The Image of the City.* Cambridge, Massachusetts: The MIT Press, 1960. Print.
Rosenberg, Karen. "Art That Interacts If You Interface." *The New York Times* July 29, 2011, sec. Arts: C23. Print.
Walter, Ekaterina. "What Your Conference Room Names Say About Your Company Culture." Inc. by Mansueto Ventures. 2014. Web. December 2017.
Weiser, Mark. "The Computer for the 21st Century." *Scientific American* 1991: 66. Print.

CHAPTER 2: SENSORY STIMULATION

London: Selfridges "Selfridges Says 'Switch Off' with No Noise." London, Selfridges & Co, 2013. Print.
"The 'Magic Threshold': Milan's New Gateway to the World." *SEA and Culture.* SEA Group. Web. June 2017.
"Threshold." *Collins English Dictionary-Complete and Unabridged.* 12th ed. HarperCollins Publishers, 2014. Print.
Block, Annie. "Listen and Learn." *Interior Design* March 2010: 92–94. Print.
Cavendish, Richard. "Mar 15 1909: The Opening of Selfridge's Department Store." *History Today* 2009: 12. Print.
CNN Travel Staff. "Will Shoppers Kindly Shut Up? Selfridges Launches 'Silence Room'." *Travel.* CNN. 2013. Web. May 2017.
Glass, Tamie. "Experiential Interiors: Feeling Space." Proc. of IDEC 2013 Annual Conference, Indianapolis. 443–46. Print.
Glass, Tamie. "Experiential Interiors: Hearing Space." *Design with Intelligence.* Proc. of IDEC 2011 Annual Conference, Denver. 236–38. Print.
Hart, Sara. "Neues Tempodrom: Berlin, Germany." *Architectural Record* October (2003): 126–29. Print.
Jilani, Sarah. "Natural Urbanism: The Feeling Environments of Simon Heijdens." AnOther Publishing Ltd. 2016. Web. April 2018.
Kaplan, Stephen. "The Restorative Benefits of Nature: Toward an Integrative Framework." *Journal of Environmental Psychology* 15.3 (1995): 169–82. Print.
Mays, Vernon. "Old School, New School: University of Virginia." *Architect Magazine* 2008. Print.
Nute, Kevin. "How to Stay Calmer, More Alert and Save the Environment: Bring the Weather Indoors." *Health & Science.* The Washington Post August 14, 2017. Web. October 2017.
Nute, Kevin. "The Next Step in Sustainable Design: Bringing the Weather Indoors." *Environment + Energy.* The Conversation US, Inc. July 12, 2017. Web. October 2017.
Nutter, Forrest W. Jr. *Encyclopedia of Research Design.* Weber-Fechner Law. Thousand Oaks, California SAGE Publications, Inc., 2012. Print.
Parafianowicz, Lydia. "On Tension by Eva Malschaert." Frame Magazine 2011. Web. July 2011.
Stratford, Oli. "Silence Room by Alex Cochrane." Disegno-Daily by Disegno. 2013. Web. April 2018.
Ulrich, Roger S. "View through a Window May Influence Recovery from Surgery." *Science* 224.4647 (1984): 420–22. Print.
Wade, Derry. "Sound Lounge Provides Auditory and Visual Connections for U.Va. School of Architecture Community." Rector and Visitors of the University of Virginia. 2010. Web. January 2011.
Wohlwill, Joachim F. "The Physical Environment: A Problem for a Psychology of Stimulation." *Journal of Social Issues* 22.4 (1966): 29–38. Print.

CHAPTER 3: HARMONIOUS INTEGRATION

"Choice Overload." Behavioral Science Solutions Ltd. 2018. Web. April 2018.
"Class, Can I Have Your Attention?" *360 Magazine* 2015: 3–16. Print.
"De Hogeweyk: Village for People with Dementia." *Lost in Space: Architecture and Dementia.* Eds. Feddersen, Eckhard, and Insa Lüdtke. Basel: Birkhäuser, 2014. 176–81. Print.
"Interactive Learning Space Initiative." Ball State University. 2017. Web. June 2017.
"Richland College Adds Steelcase Learnlab." Steelcase Inc. 2012. Web. May 2017.
"Sherwin-Williams Introduces Colorsnap®, an Integrated Color Selection System." SpecialChem. 2015. Web. June 2017.
"Situation." Dictionary.com, LLC. Web. April 2018.
"Steelcase Introduces Learnlab(Tm) Environments." Steelcase Inc., 2007. Print.
The Hogeweyk: Background and Vision. Netherlands: Vivium Hogewey: The Hogeweyk, 2016. Print.
Aguilar, Mario. "This Table Listens to Your Boring Meetings and Pulls out the Good Stuff." Gizmodo Media Group. 2015. Web. June 2017.
Barker, Roger G. "Behavior Settings: Defining Attributes and Varying Properties." *Ecological Psychology: Concepts and Methods for Studying the Environment of Human Behavior.* Stanford, California: Stanford University Press, 1968. 18–34. Print.
Brick, Jason. "A Listening Table That Highlights a Meeting's Best Parts." PSFK LLC. 2015. Web. June 2017.
Brownlee, James. "The New York Times Invents a Confer-

ence Table That Takes Notes for You." Co.Design by Mansueto Ventures. 2015. Web. June 2017.
Canter, David. "Children in Hospital: A Facet Theory Approach to Person/Place Synomorphy." *Journal of Architectural Research* 6.2 (1977): 20–32. Print.
Goetz, Kaomi. "How Steelcase Redesigned the 21st Century College Classroom." Co.Design by Mansueto Ventures 2010. Web. June 2017.
Gupta, Sanjay. "Dementia Village." *CNN's World's Untold Stories*. YouTube LLC. November 16, 2013. Web. November 2017.
Kim, Sheila. "Sherwin-Williams' Colorsnap Aims to Simplify Paint Selection." Architizer, Inc. Web. June 2017.
Lawson, Bryan. *The Language of Space*. Boston, Massachusetts: Architectural Press, 2001. Print.
Lufkin, Bryan. "Maker Profile: The New York Times R&D Lab." Maker Media, Inc. 2015. Web. June 2017.
Magnusson, David. "Wanted: A Psychology of Situations." *Toward a Psychology of Situations: An Interactional Perspective*. Hillsdale, New Jersey: Lawrence Erlbaum Associates, Inc., 1981. 9–35. Print.
Morgan, Jacob. "Say Goodbye to Knowledge Workers and Welcome to Learning Workers." Forbes Media LLC 2016. Web. June 2017.
Ross, Johanna Agerman. "Konstantin Grcic on Silicon Valley." DesignDaily by Disegno 2015. Web. June 2016.
Rupprecht, Isabelle. "Dementia Village 'De Hogeweyk' in Weesp." *DETAIL* 2012. Print.
Sommer, Robert. "Shopping at the Co-Op." *Journal of Environmental Psychology* 18.1 (1998): 45–53. Print.
Steelcase. *Active Learning Spaces: Insights, Applications, and Solutions*. Steelcase Inc., 2015. 13–49. Print.
Tucker, Emma. "Karl Lenton Designs Egg-Shaped Movable Therapy Pods for Prisons." Dezeen Ltd. 2015. Web. June 2017.
Weller, Chris. "Inside the Dutch 'Dementia Village' That Offers Beer, Bingo, and Top-Notch Healthcare." Business Insider Inc. 2017. Web. November 2017.

CHAPTER 4: INTERACTIVE TRANSACTION

"Clūnēs – Remodeling Your Living Body." *Projects*. Copenhagen Institute of Interaction Design. 2015. Web. November 2017.
"Luminescent Wood Brings Wonder to Children's Hospital." St. Kilda, Australia: ENESS, 2016. Print.
"Reset by UNStudio and SCAPE." Archello. 2017. Web. November 2017.
"Reset Stress Reduction Pods @ Salone Del Mobile." YouTube LLC. 2018. Web. April 2018.
Ahlquist, Sean, Leah Ketcheson, and Constanza Colombi. "Multisensory Architecture: The Dynamic Interplay of Environment, Movement and Social Function." *Architectural Design* 87.2 (2017): 90–99. Print.
Brownell, Blaine. "Materials Research with a Social Focus." *Technology*. Architect Magazine by Hanley Wood Media, Inc. 2016. Web. November 2017.
Bullivant, Lucy. *Responsive Environments: Architecture, Art and Design*. London: V&A Contemporaries, Victoria & Albert Museum, 2006. Print.
Caan, Shashi. *Rethinking Design and Interiors: Human Beings in the Built Environment*. London: Laurence King Publishing Ltd, 2011. Print.
Cilento, Karen. "Roll It Experimental Housing / University of Karlsruhe." ArchDaily. 2011. Web. November 2017.
ENESS. *Lumes: Naturally Led Catalog*. St. Kilda, Australia: ENESS. Print.
Fell, Robert David. "Wood in the Human Environment: Restorative Properties of Wood in the Built Indoor Environment." University of British Columbia, 2010. Print.
Moore, Gary T. "Environment, Behaviour and Society: A Brief Look at the Field and Some Current EBS Research at the University of Sydney." Proc. of 6th International Conference of the Environment-Behavior Research Association, China. Tianjin, China: Baihua Literature and Art Publishing House, 2004. 489–506. Print.
Pavitt, Jane. *Brilliant: Lights & Lighting*. London: V&A Publications, 2004. Print.
Pyykkönen, Melina. "The Smart Chair That Wants to Save Your Life." SPACE10. 2017. Web. November 2017.
Rajagopal, Avinash. "Milan Exhibit Asks: Can an Office Bring Joy?" Metropolis. Web. January 2018.
Reinalter, Sandra. "Roll It." DETAIL. 2009. Web. August 2017.
Sommer, Robert. "Sociofugal Space." *American Journal of Sociology* 72.6 (1967): 654–60. Print.
Wapner, Seymour. "Transactions of Persons-in-Environments: Some Critical Transitions." *Journal of Environmental Psychology* 1 (1981): 223–39. Print.

CHAPTER 5: SPATIAL TRANSFORMATION

"How to Harness Architectural Metals' Living Finish for Impactful Design." 2016. Web. April 2018.
"Look Airbnb Welcomes You to Its 3D Home." Lighthouse Independent Media Pte Ltd. 2015. Web. April 2018.
"Welcome Home." Spikes Asia. Web. April 2018.
"Why Virtual Reality Is Set to Transform Mental Health Treatment." Careers in Psychology.org. Web. April 2018.
Averill, James R. "Personal Control Over Aversive Stimuli and Its Relationship to Stress." *Psychological Bulletin* 80.4 (1973): 286–303. Print.
Borgobello, Bridget. "Softshelter Provides Disaster Relief Housing with a Personal Touch." Gizmag Pty Ltd. 2011. Web. April 2018.
Brand, Stewart. "Built for Change." *How Buildings Learn: What Happens after They're Built*. New York: Penguin Group, 1994. 190–209. Print.
Brand, Stewart. "The Romance of Maintenance." *How Buildings Learn: What Happens after They're Built*. New York: Penguin Group, 1994. 110–31. Print.
Depledge, M. H., R. J. Stone, and W. J. Bird. "Can Natural and Virtual Environments Be Used to Promote Human Health and Wellbeing?" *Environmental Science & Technology* 45 (2011): 4660–65. Print.
Ferrara, Marinella, and Murat Bengisu. "Materials That Change Color: Chemochromic Materials." *Materials That Change Color: Smart Materials, Intelligent Design*. New York: Springer, 2013. 45–47. Print.
Gomes, Rute. "Future Design for a Flexible Use of the Dwelling." Technical University of Lisbon, 2017. Print.
Gorini, Alessandra, and Giuseppe Riva. "The Potential of Virtual Reality as Anxiety Management Tool: A Randomized Controlled Study in a Sample of Patients Affected by Generalized Anxiety Disorder." *Trials* 9.25 (2008): 1–9. Print.
Graham, Lindsay T., Carson J. Sandy, and Samuel D. Gosling. "Manifestations of Individual Differences in Physical and Virtual Environments." *The Wiley-Blackwell Handbook of Individual Differences*. Eds. Chamorro-Premuzic, Tomas, Sophie von Stumm, and Adrian Furnham. Hoboken, New Jersey: Blackwell Publishing Ltd., 2011. 773–800. Print.
Idemen, A. Esra, Emrah Acar, and S. Meert Şener. "Assessing the Adaptive Re-Use Potential of Buildings in

Emergencies: Analysis of Architectural Design Factors." Proc. of Architecture in Emergency: Re-thinking the Refugee Crisis, İstanbul Kültür University, Faculty of Architecture, Istanbul. 2016. 107–13. Print.

Livingston, Mark A. "Issues in Human Factor Evaluations of Augmented Reality Systems." *Human Factors in Augmented Reality Environments.* Eds. Huang, Weidong, Leila Alem, and Mark A. Livingston. New York: Springer, 2013. 3–9. Print.

Meinhold, Bridgette. "Molo Employee Tests Indoor Emergency Softshelter Made from Expandable Paper." Inhabitat 2011. Web. April 2018.

Mostafavi, Mohsen, and David Leatherbarrow. *On Weathering: The Life of Buildings in Time.* Cambridge, Massachusetts: MIT Press, 1993. Print.

Orrell, Rita Catinella. "Molo Softshelter." *Architectural Record* 2012: 51. Print.

Park, Crystal L., and Susan Folkman. "Meaning in the Context of Stress and Coping." *Review of General Psychology* 1.2 (1997): 115–44. Print.

Parker, Kate. "Sosia by Emanuele Magini for Campeggi." Dezeen Ltd. 2011. Web. January 2017.

Rice, Jennifer. "An Analysis of Interior Wood Products and Their Psychological Impact." University of British Columbia, 2004. Print.

Rockwell, David. "Unpacking Imagination." *The New York Times.* September 26, 2010, sec. Op-Chart: WK14. Print.

Senson, Alex. "Virtual Reality Therapy: Treating the Global Mental Health Crisis." Oath Tech Network 2016. Web. April 2018.

Zosh, Jennifer M., et al. "The Ultimate Block Party: Bridging the Science of Learning and the Importance of Play." *Design, Make, Play: Growing the Next Generation of Stem Innovators.* Eds. Honey, Margaret, and David E. Kanter. New York: Routledge, 2013. 95–118. Print.

Zulo, Mila. "Front Line Assembly: Experiments in Design by Front." *SOMA Magazine* 2006. Print.

CHAPTER 6: CHALLENGING PROVOCATION

Build-On: Converted Architecture and Transformed Buildings. Berlin: Die Gestalten Verlag, 2009. Print.

"Interview with Pearsonlloyd." Archisearch.gr. 2018. Web. April 2018.

"Kvadrat Textile Field 2011: Ronan & Erwan Bouroullec." Vimeo, Inc. 2012. Web. April 2018.

"Night at the Museumlaan." Archello. Web. April 2018.

"Offices of Pons + Huot / Christian Pottgiesser—Architecturespossibles." ArchDaily. 2011. Web. June 2016.

"Selexyz Dominicanen Bookstore: A Renewed 13th Century Architecture." Archilovers. 2008. Web. May 2017.

"Towards New Workplace Paradigms: Face to Face Love Seat." Teknion. Web. April 2018.

Baker, Lisa. "Night at the Museumlaan." *Temporary Architecture.* Salenstein: Braun, 2014. 60–63. Print.

Crichton-Miller, Emma. "In the Comfort of One's Museum: France's Bouroullec Brothers Warm Things up at the V&A Raphael Gallery in London." The Wall Street Journal. 2011. Web. April 2018.

Derry, Johanna. "Eating Alone: There's No Shame in a Table for One." Guardian News and Media Limited. 2013. Web. June 2017.

Hall, Edward T. "Distances in Man." *The Hidden Dimension.* New York: Anchor Books, 1969. 113–29. Print.

Hart, Anna. "New Restaurant Caters Only for Solo Diners." Independent Print Limited. 2014. Web. June 2017.

IAA Architecten. *Night at the Museumlaan.* Enschede: IAA Architecten. Print.

Olschewski, Felicitas. "Marina Van Goor." Freunde von Freunden 2013. Web. May 2017.

Schlereth, Laura. "Under the Influence." *Perspective* 2010: 7–10. Print.

Withers, Jane. "Kvadrat Textile Field." Kvadrat, 2011. Print.

ILLUSTRATION CREDITS

Andrew Meredith, copyright Selfridges 66, 67, 68–69, 70
Anna Stoltz, courtesy of Front 166 l, 166 r, 167, 168, 169
argodesign 23
Bai Jiwen, courtesy of SCA Design (a member of ONG&ONG Group) 32, 33, 34–35, 36 t, 37 t, 37 b
Charles Emerton, courtesy of Simon Heijdens 76
© Christian Gahl, courtesy of gmp Architects 79 t, 79 b, 82
© Cloud9 Architectural Photography, courtesy of SAFE Innovations Ltd 104, 105, 106 l, 106 r, 107 t
Cobbie Hill, copyright Imagination Playground LLC 178, 183 t
Copyright © SAFE Innovations Ltd 2015. All rights reserved. 107 b
Copyright and authorship—Sarah Wigglesworth, 1998 14
Copyright Dave Watson (ruislip-ha4.co.uk/koken/) 204 b
Copyright Imagination Playground LLC 183 b
Copyright PearsonLloyd 212 l, 212 r, 213 r
Copyright, Henry Dreyfuss Associates 11 t
Courtesy Antenna Design 9 l
Courtesy of Alex Cochrane Architects 71 t
Courtesy of Calzoni architetti 65 t
Courtesy of Craig Couden, *Make*: magazine 101 t
Courtesy of De Hogeweyk 123, 124–125 t, 124 b, 126 t, 126 b, 127 t, 127 b, 128 tl, 128 tr, 129
Courtesy of ENESS 146, 147 t, 147 b, 148–149, 150, 151 t, 151 b
Courtesy of Eva Malschaert 85 t, 85 b, 86, 87 t, 87 b
Courtesy of François Chambard/UM Project 102 b
Courtesy of Future-Shape GmbH 47 tl, 47 tr, 47 b, 48 t, 48 b, 49 t, 49 b
Courtesy of IAA Architects 211 b
Courtesy of IDEO 50, 51 t, 51 b, 52–53, 54 t, 54 b, 55
Courtesy of Merk X 196 b, 197 t
Courtesy of Niek Roozen BV 125 b
Courtesy of SCA Design (a member of ONG&ONG Group) 36 b
Courtesy of Simon Heijdens 72, 73, 74–75, 77 t, 77 b
Courtesy of student design team 140, 141, 142–143, 144 t, 144 b, 145 t, 145 b
Courtesy of Tim Holley 40, 41, 42 t, 42 b, 43 t, 43 b
© CPAP 198, 200 tl, 200 b, 201
dpa picture alliance / Alamy Stock Photo 83 t
Drawings by Jean Millington and Johnny Gresham, *Livable Rooms* by Inez Lovelace, published by Agricultural Extension Service and University of Tennessee, Publication 357 (reprint), March 1956. 17
Ezio Prandini, copyright campeggi srl, courtesy of Emanuele Magini 172, 173 all
giggle (https://commons.wikimedia.org/wiki/File: Maastricht_2010-03-30_-_Selexyz_Dominicanen_Dominikanerkerkstraat_1_-_panoramio_-_giggel.jpg) 196 t
Hassenzahl, Marc, et al. "Designing Moments of Meaning and Pleasure. Experience Design and Happiness." *International Journal of Design* 7.3 (2013): 26. Print. 16
Illustrations from ANATOMY FOR INTERIOR DESIGNERS by Julius Panero and Nino Repetto, copyright © 1962 by Whitney Library of Design. Used by permission of Watson-Guptill Publications, an imprint of The Crown Publishing Group, a division of Penguin Random House LLC. All rights reserved. 11 b
iStock.com/SEASTOCK 21
© Jaakko Tuomivaara 44, 45 t, 45 b
Jaap Scheeren, courtesy of MVGCA 215
Jamie Akers of the Rockwell Group, copyright Imagination Playground LLC 182
Joep Niesink, courtesy of MVGCA 214, 216 t, 216 b, 217
John Ross, courtesy of PearsonLloyd 213 l
Knoll, Inc. 9 r
Kristine Bjaadal 170, 171 t, 171 b
© Liliana Lambriev 136, 139 t, 139 b
LOOK Die Bildagentur der Fotografen GmbH / Alamy Stock Photo 80–81
© Luc Boegly, courtesy of CPAP 199, 200 tr
© Lukas Renlund (photographer) and SPACE10 137, 138 t
Material courtesy of Steelcase 117 b, 118–119, 120 t, 120 b, 121 t, 121 b
Meerkat Media 103 b
Michael Anastassiades 134, 135
Michele Nastasi Photography, courtesy of Calzoni architetti 63 t, 63 b, 64, 65 b
© Nina Heinke (illustration), Liliana Lambriev & Melina Pyykkönen (layout and concept) 138 b
No known copyright, Hermann Bopp (https://commons.wikimedia.org/wiki/File:Maastricht,_Dominicanenkerk,_bloementententoonstelling,_1899_of_1903.jpg) 197 b
No known copyright, photographer unknown (https://commons.wikimedia.org/wiki/File:1917_Allentown_High_School_Classroom_Allentown_PA.jpg) 117 t
Ori 22 t, 22 m, 22 b
Peter Bristol 38, 39 t, 39 b
Peter Marlow / Magnum Photos, courtesy of Johnson Naylor 19 l, 19 r
Photo by Mike Hensel-InMotion Studios, courtesy of Sean Ahlquist 152
Photo by Peter Matthews, courtesy of Sean Ahlquist 155 b
Photo by Sean Ahlquist 153, 154 t, 154 b
Photography and copyright Francis Dzikowski/OTTO, courtesy of François Chambard/UM Project 101 b, 102 t, 103 t
Photography and copyright GOVT 184, 185, 186, 187 t, 187 b
Photography and copyright molo 174, 175, 176 t, 176 b, 177 t, 177 b
Photography and copyright Tjeerd Derkink, courtesy of IAA Architects 207 t, 207 b, 208–209, 210 t, 210 b, 211 t
Photography by Roos Aldershoff, courtesy of Merk X 193, 194–195
Property of Joel Sanders Architect 90, 91 t, 91 b
Property of Scott Smith, courtesy of Joel Sanders Architect 88, 89, 92–93
< RESET, 2017, UNStudio © > 157, 161 b
< RESET, 2017, UNStudio © > < ©oddproduzioni > cover photo, 158–159, 160 t, 160 b, 161 t
Sean Ahlquist, University of Michigan, Photo by Gregory Wendt, Southern Illinois University—Carbondale 155 t
Sherwin-Williams 108, 109 t, 109 b
Stuart C. Wilson / Getty Images 71 b
©Studio Bouroullec & V&A Images, Victoria and Albert Museum 202, 203
Süddeutsche Zeitung Photo / Alamy Stock Photo 83 b
Suki Dhanda 204 t, 205
Tamie Glass, background dot pattern designed by starline / Freepik 24
Tamie Glass, based on diagram by Bill Moggridge. *Designing Interactions*. Cambridge, Massachusetts: The MIT Press, 2007. Print. 652. 18
Tom Moore, copyright Imagination Playground LLC 179, 180–181
© Vitra 114 t, 114 b, 115 b
© Vitra, photo: Studio AKFB 110, 111, 112–113, 115 t

ACKNOWLEDGMENTS

My first acknowledgment is to Ulrich Dangel—my friend, partner, and husband—whose unwavering faith in my work keeps me motivated and whose loving support keeps me grounded. This book would not have been possible without his constructive criticism and sensible advice, and most of all his endless patience for the considerable time commitment this type of project requires.

One textbook, in particular, has been a guide in the classroom and during the ideation phase of this book. The first edition of *Environmental Psychology for Design* introduced me to the topic, and I would like to express my appreciation to author Dak Kopec for providing this comprehensive resource. His writings on foundational theories are what inspired and informed many of the concepts presented here. Furthermore, psychologist Lindsay Graham has advanced my understanding of the connections between people and space through many thought-provoking conversations. I am grateful for her friendship, invaluable feedback, and encouragement.

Special thanks go to several former and current students for their contributions. Raquel Torres and Ronnie Marquez began exploring this topic with me during an independent study, followed by Heather Sutherland who was instrumental as a graduate research assistant. She helped with the proposal, supported the search for case studies, and corresponded with many of the contributors to obtain project documentation. Linda Kwak-Willis also served as an assistant offering a fresh perspective and an editing eye as the book continued to take shape. I am indebted to these individuals for their keen insights, especially since I hope this book will resonate with students and emerging designers.

I would like to convey my gratitude to Birkhäuser, and specifically, to the team that brought this book to fruition. Thank you to commissioning editor Henriette Mueller-Stahl who initially saw potential in my proposal, and who offered guidance throughout the writing and publishing process as the project manager. Silke Nalbach designed a user-friendly and compelling graphic layout for the book, Esther Wolfram carefully read and edited drafts of this publication, and lastly, Amelie Solbrig helped with the many production details.

A few years ago I had the good fortune to become acquainted with Susan Szenasy who wrote the foreword. While she is considered an authority on design of all scales, I particularly value her supportive yet critical stance toward the role of interiors. She serves as a touchstone for the discipline, always questioning superficiality and stressing human needs.

It is important to note that this book was made possible by generous funding from the Gene Edward Mikeska Endowed Chair for Interior Design and The University of Texas at Austin's Office of the Vice President for Research subvention grant program. I also appreciate all the designers, photographers, and companies whose work and products appear throughout this publication, and who often graciously provided materials free of charge.

Finally, I would like to express my sincere gratitude to my parents Lucille and Donny Glass who have always encouraged my creative endeavors. This book is dedicated to them.

LAYOUT, COVER DESIGN, AND TYPESETTING
Silke Nalbach, Mannheim

PROJECT MANAGEMENT
Henriette Mueller-Stahl, Berlin

COPY EDITING
Esther Wolfram, Hamburg

PRODUCTION
Amelie Solbrig, Berlin

PAPER
Multioffset, 120 g/m²

LITHOGRAPHY
LVD Gesellschaft für Datenverarbeitung mbH, Berlin

PRINTING
optimal media GmbH, Röbel, Müritz

Library of Congress Control Number: 2018937454

Bibliographic information published by the German National Library
The German National Library lists this publication in the Deutsche Nationalbibliografie; detailed bibliographic data are available on the Internet at http://dnb.dnb.de.

ISBN 978-3-0356-1193-9

e-ISBN (PDF) 978-3-0356-1060-4

P.O. Box 44, 4009 Basel, Switzerland
Part of Walter de Gruyter GmbH, Berlin/Boston

Printed on acid-free paper produced from chlorine-free pulp. TCF ∞

Printed in Germany

ISBN 978-3-0356-1193-9

9 8 7 6 5 4 3 2 1 www.birkhauser.com